Method and Mysticism

Method and Mysticism

Cosmos, Nature and Environment in Islamic Mysticism

Seyyed Shahabeddin Mesbahi

FONS VITAE

First published in 2011 by
Fons Vitae
49 Mockingbird Valley Drive
Louisville, KY 40207
http://www.fonsvitae.com

Library of Congress Control Number: 2011939592
ISBN 9781891785863

Cover Picture: Tomb of Khwāja Shams al-Dīn
Muḥammad Ḥāfiẓ Shirāzī (d. 792 AH/1390 CE),
the great Persian mystic and poet, Shiraz, Iran.

This book was typeset by Neville Blakemore, Jr.

Printed in Canada

This book is dedicated to my parents with humble gratitude.

Table of Contents

Table of Contents, continued

Introduction: Towards a Methodology in Approaching Islamic Mysticism

The issues of nature, the environment and the cosmos as a whole are of increasing concern not only to environmentalists, but to the general public, and to scholars, policy-makers, and theologians alike. In this regard, Islamic scholars have not remained aloof from discussions or debates over these issues. In fact, within the Islamic mystical tradition, these concepts are repeatedly alluded to and form part of the core of the mystical experience. Their elevation in the Islamic mystical tradition fosters an attitude that surpasses respect for the concepts in and of themselves, and views them as manifestations of the Absolute.

The work at hand intends to elaborate on the concepts of cosmos, nature and environment in Islamic mysticism. Despite the extensive studies on cosmos, nature and the environment, there is an evident gap in the literature dealing with these concepts from a mystical perspective. While the manuscript will utilize these and other existing scholarly works, it will rely primarily on original sources, namely the Qur'ān and the works of Islamic mystics.

In addition to a dearth of scholarship, we also face methodological problems and limitations in that conventional and prevailing methodology prevents an in depth study of religious "experiences" in general, and mystical experiences in particular. Here, we should address shortly a general misapplication of the concept of "experience" among some contemporary scholars of religious studies.

This misapplication, in my view, is the general result of employing the Hobbesian approach to "experience," in the field of religious studies. Thomas Hobbes (1588-1679) wrote in *The Elements of Law*:

> The remembrance of the succession of one thing to another, that is, of what *antecedent*, and what *consequent*, and what *concomitant* is called an experiment...To have had many experiments, is that we call *experience*, which is nothing else but remembrance of what antecedents have been followed with what consequents...Experience concludeth nothing universally.[1] [emphasis added]

Although a "Hobbesian definition of experience" (which I have termed the Hobbesian triangle) [Figure 1], could be a useful tool in its related social/political aspects, because of its mechanical nature (antecedent, consequent and concomitant), it may not be applied successfully and effectively as an approach to the religious, and especially mystical experience. An example of implementing this mechanical method of understanding can be found in Ninian Smart's approach to "religion and ideology" as world view analysis by applying the idea of *epoche'*. According to Smart,

> The *most important idea* in modern social science was that of *epoche'* or suspension of judgment. In other words, you suspend your own beliefs about others (whether that be culture, or group, or person) in order to make your description more realistic.[2][emphasis added]

Smart then concludes,

> The study of *religions and ideologies* can be called world view analysis. In this way we try to depict the history and nature of the symbols and beliefs that have helped form the structure of human consciousness and society. *This is the heart of the modern study of religion.*[3] [emphasis added]

The main paradox in Smart's observation springs from his dependence on *epoche'* as an essential accessory to construct a world view through observation of "religions and ideologies." Observation of "religions and ideologies" in the same container of dialectical inquiry, by itself contradicts the *epoche'*. In other words, despite all their differences such as roots, realms and doctrines, observation of these two in a homogenous position, shows that Smart did not apply the rule of *epoche'*, i.e., the suspension of judgment, in order to reach a more realistic description of the subject.

Although, Smart does not point to the exact same origin for both "ideology and religion," his mechanical method in observing "religions and ideologies" both simultaneously *and* in the same category to reach a world view as if they were the product of the same origin, leads to the *desacralization* of religious traditions/experiences. As a result, a large expanse of religious experiences will be sliced into separate and disconnected *performances*; performances that are not recognized and dignified with respect to the characteristics and identity of the religious/mystical experiences. Suffice it to say that such experiences forfeit their organic religious/mystical identity.

In contemporary scholarship on Islamic mysticism, one

can recognize a lack of awareness of an organic identity (*huwiyah*) which is embedded in each mystical concept. This identity consists of numerous elements which cannot be elaborated in a one-dimensional approach. Each term, metaphor, or recorded saying of Sufi masters carries within itself affinities with different elements in the long tradition of Islamic mysticism. Underestimating the coherent connections of these affinities and simply translating a mystical term would not shed light upon the organic identity of Islamic mystical concepts.

Mysticism utilizes its own language, terminologies and tenets to examine the place of cosmos, nature and the environment and provides us with a more comprehensive understanding of these concepts. Islamic mysticism (*'irfān*) provides us with the opportunity to observe and discover the presence of mystical metaphors and allegories and to unveil the very essence of the intermeshed physical and spiritual characteristics of nature, environment and cosmos. The concept of "experience" in Islamic mysticism, has an "organic" rather than a mechanical "identity." This identity needs to be elaborated with respect to its organic affinities and interconnectedness with its own concepts of "tradition" and "sanctity" as the main domain of Islamic mystical experience. This elaboration will be applied by introducing a new and organic approach which I have termed a "methodological triangle."

The New Methodological Triangle and its Related Concepts

This study suggests that this new methodological triangle be used as a methodological tool for the analysis of each mystical concept in Islamic mysticism. This triangle consists of three dimensions of *sanctity*, *tradition* and *experience* [Figure 2]. These three dimensions are all in constant and mutual relation and affinity. Observation of an Islamic mystical concept within this organic triangle, will help us comprehend some dimensions of the "organic identity" of each Islamic mystical concept. In order to avoid generalization and to reach a proper understanding of Islamic mystical concepts, each concept has to be considered within the context of its constant junction with the three dimensions of the triangle without disregarding the consistent affinities between sanctity, tradition and experience.

The main goal of this work, i.e., to illustrate the place and importance of the "cosmos, nature and environment in Islamic mysticism," is here discussed within the context of the suggested methodological triangle [Figure 3]. A proper approach to Islamic mystical concepts can be achieved by taking into account the interdependence between the three dimensions of the organic triangle.

The term "tradition" here refers to the Islamic mystical tradition which consists of different dimensions such as mystical doctrines, history, etymology, culture, and the local peculiarities of mystical fraternities. The long history of the

Islamic mystical tradition starts with the Qur'ān. In other words, the Qur'ān is the first source and the foundation of the Islamic mystical tradition. Without having the essentiality of the Qur'ān in mind no research around the tradition of Islamic mysticism will be complete. The essential concepts, doctrines, terminologies, metaphors, and different categorizations such as states (*aḥwāl*) and stations (*maqāmāt*) of the mystical path have been derived by Islamic mystics of different eras, from the contents of the Qur'ān. The second major source of Islamic mysticism is the "tradition of the Prophet Muḥammad" (his recorded sayings, deeds, actions, and personality). He is considered by Islamic mystics to be the "first and peerless master" (*murshid-i awwal* and *murshid-i a'lā*) and "the most elevated example of the universal/perfect human being"(*al-insān al-kāmil*). In addition to Prophetic tradition, the tradition of the Shi'ī Imams and the Prophet's daughter Fāṭimah have also been incorporated into Shi'ī *'irfān*.[4]

By the term "sanctity" I mean the sacred surroundings of the mystical experience as it is understood in Islamic mysticism. Sanctity for the Islamic mystics, is the absolute presence of the Absolute. For the Islamic mystic there is no realm of existence save the "presence (*ḥaḍra*) of the Absolute Existence." As will be described later, "sanctity" (the manifestation of the Absolute), for the Islamic mystics is *both* the whole existence of the mystic and the only domain of (and for) the mystical experience. This mystical realization of sanctity is the result of the Islamic mystics' profound awareness of *tawḥīd* (the Unity of the Absolute) as the first doctrine of Islam. The whole of existence, for the Islamic mystic, is one manifestation of the One as "His sacred presence"(sanctity). The mystic lives, experiences and intuits *within* the sacredness of His presence (*ḥaḍra*). The concept of sanctity, because of its essential doctrinal source (which is *tawḥīd* or the Unity of the Absolute) is one of the most important characteristics of the Islamic mystical tradition which has to be separately considered in each approach to the Islamic mystical concepts.

By the third dimension of the triangle, i.e. "experience," we are referring to the mystical experiences as the ways which have been described by the Sufi masters. Experience of each mystical state (*ḥāl*) and station (*maqām*), in the words of the mystics, also conveys the position and place of those states and stations in the organic categories of the "mystical path" (*ṭarīqa*). In this observation we can also discern a proper utilization of the mystical terms and expressions and their place in the mystical path.

To show the proper function of the triangle and purposefulness/directionality of the mystical experience towards the Absolute, I utilize the concept of *istirjā'* (seeking perpetual return towards the Absolute) [Figure 4]. The return to the Absolute, for the Islamic mystics, is the goal of each experience. The more advanced an experience is, the more successful and exalted the return that can be achieved. This return, which is eternal for the Islamic mystic, is the reality of the experience. Regarding the centrality of the concept of "return" in Islamic mysticism and its connection with all three dimensions of the triangle, I will employ this concept as the *examiner*.

The process of "return" takes place via the "mystical path" (*ṭarīqa*) which consists of different *states* (*aḥwāl*) and *stations* (*maqāmāt*). In simple terms, "state" (*ḥāl*) is an instantaneous mystical bestowal from the Absolute for the mystic. It will not last for long and the mystic has not the power to lure that gift or to reside in it. On the other hand, station (*maqām*), is an enduring mystical stage and is the result of the mystic's endeavor. As the 13th century Persian Sufi master Rūmī states : "*ḥāl* (state) is like the [one] manifestation of the [face] of [that] beautiful bride and [this] *maqām* (station) [resembles] being [alone or in the private intimacy] with the bride."[5]

Among the stations of the "mystical path" (*ṭarīqa*), the two stations of *annihilation* and *subsistence* (*fanā'* and *baqā'*, respectively) are considered by many Islamic mystics to be the ultimate stations of the mystical path. The study employs these two stations as the *framework* through which the concepts of cosmos, nature, and environment are analyzed. Therefore, the focus is on the cosmic, natural and environmental examples which reveal the "experiences" and explanations of the Islamic masters with respect to these two major mystical stations [Figure 5]. Such an approach not only provides us with the opportunity to observe some important aspects of the mystical interpretation of Islamic masters, it proves also instrumental in avoiding generalization by facilitating concentration on the specific analytical framework of study. With this framework, the pattern of the triangle—regarding the goal of this study—is *completed* and we can view the triangle with all of its main components. [Figure 6].

Looking at the variety of approaches among mystics of different eras, I will also try to show how their specific interpretation of natural, environmental and cosmic elements fits their individual approach to the different *states* (*aḥwāl*) and *stations* (*maqāmāt*) of the mystical path. We will also be able to pinpoint a series of differentiations in the interpretations and perspectives of Islamic mystics. The analysis will show how, stemming from the sources of Islamic mysticism, the mystical allegories and metaphors construct the mystical manifestations of cosmos, nature and environment.

The aim here is to analyze the methodology of selected and well-known Islamic mystics of different eras, such as Ḥallāj, Ibn 'Arabī, Rūzbihān Baqlī Shirāzī and Rūmī.

In the first chapter, the primary concern will be on the works of Islamic masters of different eras and their interpretations of "cosmos, nature and environment". I will also explain some important metaphors, allegories (such as light) and ideas (such as constant re-creation or *khalq-i mudām*). The suggested triangle will be employed in the analysis of the works (mainly experiences) of Islamic masters. This chapter will provide us with the *general view* of the triangle with its relevance to the concepts of cosmos, nature and the environment. The second chapter, which is divided into two sections, is devoted primarily to the discussion of the concept of "return" as the examiner (or evaluator) of the suggested triangle, to show its implications for the concepts of cosmos, nature and environment. This discussion has been contextualized within a critical analysis of Annemarie Schimmel, Emile Durkheim and Toshihiko Izutsu and their approach to the concepts of tradition, sanctity and experience. This chapter will provide us with a *more specific view* of the triangle with its relevance to the cosmos, nature and environment.

Chapter I

Cosmos, Nature, and Environment in Islamic Mysticism: An Overview

This chapter addresses the perceptions of the three concepts of cosmos, nature and the environment, within the mystical experiences of annihilation and subsistence or *fanā'* and *baqā'*. As the Qur'ān is the essential, primordial source from which Islamic mystical concepts are extracted, the chapter begins with an examination of a Qur'ānic example, in which the "tree" is used as a metaphor for understanding the cosmos as a whole. The approaches of 'Allāmah Ṭabāṭabāī and Abū Ḥamid Al-Ghazālī toward this doctrinal example provide a guide for understanding its complexities and relevance. This investigation then turns toward the experiences of *fanā'* and *baqā'* of prominent Islamic figures, such as Ḥusayn ibn Manṣur al-Ḥallāj, Bāyazīd Basṭāmī, Al-Ghazālī, Rūzbihān Baqlī Shirāzī, Muḥyiddīn Ibn 'Arabī, Jalāl al-Dīn Rūmī and the relevance of the concepts of cosmos, nature and the environment in their experiences.

The concept of "light" as an essential allegory in Islamic mysticism, and the concept of "constant re-creation" (*khalq-i mudām*) of the cosmos are followed by the idea of transubstantial motion (*ḥarakat al-jawharia*) in the thought of the prominent philosopher and mystic Mullā Ṣadrā.

The discussion around the concept of the "universal/perfect human being" (*al-insān al-kāmil*) as one of the most prominent concepts in Islamic mysticism and its cosmic aspects connect us to the last part of this chapter where we look at some of the important natural, cosmic and environmental symbols and allegories in Islamic mysticism.

1. A Qur'ānic doctrinal example

In Islamic mysticism, stones, mountains, emeralds, rubies, springs and dust, as well as the sun, the moon, the stars, and the rain, all represent cosmic and natural manifestations or effusions of the One and serve as delicate metaphors for the encounter with the infinite presence of the Real. Such metaphors are directly revealed by the Qur'ān and are fully nourished by the Islamic tradition.

> The outward manifestation (*ẓāhir*) of the Qur'ān resembles the human being (*nafs-i ādamī*) Whose features are manifested (*ẓāhir*) but whose soul is concealed (*khafī*).[6]

For the mystic (*'ārif*), nobility and bounty of faith, which are the fruits of perfect intentions and deeds, are cultivated in every instance of life as opportunities for tasting a new spiritual intimacy with the presence of the Absolute. This view is well illustrated in the following Qur'ānic verse which represents a doctrinal approach to the cosmos and relies on the allegory of the tree, a natural symbol:

> Seest thou not how Allāh sets forth a parable? A goodly Word is like a goodly tree, whose root is firmly fixed and its branches (reach) to the heavens. It brings forth its fruit at all times, by the leave of its Lord. So Allāh sets forth parables for men in order that they may receive admonition. (14:24,25)

A goodly word (*kalimat'un ṭayyibah*) is symbolized by a goodly tree (*shajarat'un tayyibah*). Its roots (*aṣl*) are firmly connected with the ultimate certainty of Unity (*tawḥīd*), and therefore, with the essence of True Knowledge. This tree brings the believers an infinite succession of tastes or manifestations of the One Truth.

In contrast to this, the evil word and the evil tree degrade the noble Truth of the essential source. Such a tree is limp and cannot reach the elevation, loftiness and the protracted movement toward the eternal orchard of celestial Reality.

> And the parable of the evil word is that of an evil tree.
> It is torn up by the root from the surface of the earth.
> It has no stability. (Qur'ān, 14:26)

Allāmah Muḥammad Ḥusayn Ṭabāṭabā-ī (1892-1981), a prominent Shi'ī scholar, in his magnum opus, *Al-Mizān*, considers the goodly word to be a proclamation of God's Unity, a firm principle that is protected and guarded from change, decline and invalidity. This root will provide the branches and fruits of noble knowledge, praiseworthy morals (virtues) and perfect deeds, which nourish the believer. On the other hand, any word or action, that is contrary to this universal process of perfection, yields no fruits.[7]

In another Qur'ānic verse, this interconnected hierarchy is described as the ascendence of goodly sayings and deeds towards God: "...To him mount up (all) Words of Purity. It is He who exalts each deed of righteousness..." (35:10).

By understanding the continuous movement toward perfection indicated in numerous Qur'ānic examples, Islamic mystics have delineated the ascending states (*aḥwāl*) and stations (*maqāmāt*) such as *tawbah* (repentance), *riḍā* (contentment), *ṣabr* (patience) *ḥayrah* (astonishment) and *yaqīn* (certainty).

Abū Ḥāmid al-Ghazālī (d. 504/1111) relies on the above mentioned (35:10) Qur'ānic verse when he illustrates the purifying love and the appearance of its fruits in the heart, tongue and limbs as the "good tree whose root is firm and whose branches are in the sky."[8]

In other words, as a goodly word (proclamation to the "Absolute's Unity" or *tawḥīd*) appears in the mystic's life, the manifestation of the goodly word, divulges itself in both the physical and spiritual dimensions of his/her life. The goodly word, as practiced by the mystic, benefits both his/her body and soul. Both the esoteric and exoteric components of the mystic's life will be encompassed by this proclamation (goodly word), and will guide the mystic toward the more transparent presence of the Absolute. This process points to the reality of constant return towards the Absolute. This eternal process of return in its ultimate stages, turns the reality of the mystic to the goodly word itself. In the ultimate stage, the mystic's whole existence becomes his/her absolute proclamation to the Unity of the Absolute (*tawḥīd*) as he/she ascends toward Him as the symbolic good tree ascends and extends its branches to the sky, i.e., in the direction of the Absolute.

It is worth mentioning that Jesus (who has been mentioned by different Sufi masters, as an example of the perfect human being (*insān al-kāmil*) and the guide "*murshid*" in the mystical path), is referred to in the Qur'ān (3:45) as the *kalimah* (the Word of God). This title contributes to the mystical understanding of the goodly word. A perfect human being (*insān al-kāmil*) who represents the goodly word (the proclamation to the Absolute's Unity) is like a goodly tree which is in the path of consistent return and ascendence towards the Absolute. In a greater scale, the perfect human being as the goodly tree represents the whole cosmos which through one declaration, proclaims the goodly word (the reality of *tawḥīd* or Unity of the Absolute) and returns towards Him. The cosmos, for the Islamic mystic, appears as a single Word of the Absolute and the perfect/universal human being (*insān al-kāmil*), manifests the perfect image of the Word.

Ghazālī in his mystical interpretation uses the symbolism of the tree also to exemplify the mystical annihilation (*fanā'*) and subsistence (*baqā'*), which occur in the symbolic tree as a sign of perpetual creation. Each new taste or new epiphany of the eternal Truth is completed by the next image. In the higher stations, the mystic is perpetually annihilated by a glimpse of the Absolute's manifestations (i.e., attains the mystical annihilation or *fanā'*), and in turn subsists in the very next image of the Absolute's Existence (i.e., achieves the mystical subsistence or *baqā'*). The mystic becomes annihilated from his/her very previous awareness (the totality of his/her awareness of the proximity and presence of the Absolute *or* the previous manifestation of the Absolute) and embraces the new manifestation of the Absolute and resides and subsists in it (i.e., the station of subsistence).

Depending on the awareness of the mystic of the new manifestations and his/her spiritual capability, the experience of these two stations will continue again. The mystic again becomes annihilated from his/her previous awareness (the previous Absolute's manifestation) in which he/she has subsisted, and again will subsist in the new epiphany of the Absolute. In the stations of annihilation and subsistence, sanctity, which is present in each manifestation of the Absolute, is the domain of mystical "experience." The mystic's awareness of the sanctified domain of his/her mystical experience (the Absolute's manifestation), helps him/her to attain a more transparent awareness of *tawḥīd* (the Unity of the Absolute). Mystical annihilation and subsistence (*fanā'* and *baqā'*) are not contradictory, but rather embrace and compliment each other.

2. Mystical Texts and Masters: on Cosmos, Nature and Environment

We now turn to the mystical works of a few Islamic masters of different eras to see how they have used nature and the environment to symbolically depict their experiences of *fanā'* and *baqā'*, and to analyze their perception of mystical awareness of the cosmos and its ties with the environment and with the Real.

Ḥusayn ibn Manṣūr al-Ḥallāj

Ḥusayn ibn Manṣūr al-Ḥallāj (d. 309/922), the famous Persian mystic, was executed mainly due to his utterance, *ana'l ḥaqq*. Many jurisprudents pronounced him an apostate and he was hung during the reign of the 'Abbāsid caliph al-Muqtadir. His well known expression, "*ana'l ḥaqq*" (I am the Real) is one of the most controversial mystical claims. He has been mentioned by Islamic mystics as the symbol of martyrdom through the station of mystical annihilation (*fanā'*).

We might state that in his view, the annihilation of "I" constantly occurs in "Reality." This process embraces the constant annihilation of annihilation and *baqā'*. In the station of annihilation (*fanā' al fanā'*), "I," in each domain of manifestation, becomes more and more purified and faces the new horizons of eternal life in *baqā'* (subsistence). In the station of annihilation (*fanā'*), when the mystic is in the constant awareness of the coming manifestations of the Absolute, he/she will have the opportunity to extend the experience of annihilation and subsistence (*baqā'*). In this advanced station, the mystic does not remain in his/her first experience of annihilation, but he/she renews it again. In the experience of *fanā' al-fanā'* (annihilation of annihilation), the mystic becomes annihilated from his/her previous annihilation and subsists in the new manifestation of the Absolute (station of subsistence). In other words, the mystic experiences a new phase of reality of the whole existence.

In the continuation of the experience of *fanā'* and *baqā'*, the mystic in each experience unveils the hidden reality of the whole cosmos. The term *ḥijāb* (veil) in its mystical understanding, points to the layers of realities (*ḥaqā'iq*) which have been veiled because of the forgetfulness (*ghaflah*) of individuals of the "presence of the Absolute" (the sanctity of the Absolute's manifestations). In any genuine mystical experience, the mystic will be able to see some portion of the unveiled realities of entities in the cosmos.

These first types of mystical unveiling could be very partial and inconsistent . The term "partial awareness" (*ishrāf-i juz'ī*) may be appropriate here which includes different levels of awareness. In the experience of *fanā'*, which is associated with *baqā'*, because of the very advanced nature of the experience, the mystic sees some unveiled realities of the whole cosmos in a large scale.

In each experience of mystical annihilation and subsistence (*fanā'* and *baqā'*), one layer of the cosmos as a whole intermeshed and connected reality, becomes unveiled to the mystic. This I call "cosmic awareness" (*ishrāf-i kullī*) which also consists of its own levels of awareness. In experiencing *fanā'* and *baqā'*, the process of "unveiling of the essences or substances of the entities" (*kashf al-dhawāt*), enters a cosmic level. When the experience of *fanā'* and *baqā'* continues (station of *fanā' al-fanā'* or annihilation of annihilation associated with subsistence or *baqā'*), the mystic obtains a more vivid awareness of the whole cosmos. The new manifestations of the Absolute (Light of the Absolute Reality), remove the darkness of forgetfulness (*ghaflah*) from the heart of the mystic and the mystic sees a clearer face of the cosmic realities. From this different process of unveiling, comes the expression "eye of the heart" (*'ayn al-qalb* or *chashm-i dil*). The mystic sees the hidden substance of the entities through his/her unveiled heart.

Ḥallāj's awareness, i.e. his intense experience in the station of annihilation of annihilation (*fanā' al-fanā'*) associated with *baqā'* (subsistence), may have been the cause of his public utterance. His controversial phrase, "I am the Real" (*ana'l ḥaqq*), as understood by later Sufi tradition, conveys a completely different meaning. The mystic in the very advanced and constant experience of annihilation and subsistence is blessed by the gift of the ceaseless process of unveiling, and witnesses the consistent renewal of the whole cosmos in the Light of the Absolute Reality. In this exalted process, the mystic sees absolutely nothing save the constant self-disclosures (*tajallīyāt*) of the Absolute. In other words, he sees everything in its very true reality (unveiled from the multiple veils). The mystic sees the journey of the whole unveiled cosmos in the path of return towards the Absolute. At this station, the mystic becomes aware of his reality as the torchbearer of this return and sees (through "the eye of the heart"), his very manifest (*ẓāhir*) reality as the noblest self-disclosure of the Absolute. Thus, the mystic comes to a truthful mystical awareness of his/her very existence. The essence of that awareness is that his/her whole reality comes from the Absolute Reality (i.e., he is non-existence within the Presence of the Absolute Existence). The mystic becomes truly aware of the fact that his reality is in constant return towards the Absolute. The mystical certainty (*yaqīn*) of this essential awareness leads him to such a mystical utterance as *ana'l ḥaqq* (I am the Real).

In another translation, this phrase would be translated as "I am theTruth." The word "*Ḥaqq*" as one of the Absolute's Names means also "the Truth." The mystic proclaims that the Absolute is the only true, worthy and deserving Source for the return.

Ḥallāj declares his longing for *fanā'* by relying on the Qur'ānic expressions (102:5,7 and 56:95) of *'ilm al-yaqīn*—knowledge of certitude—*'ayn al-yaqīn*—vision of certitude or essence of certainty—and *ḥaqq al-yaqīn*—the real certitude. Using the symbolism of the moth and the light of the candle, he reveals the different levels of mystical certainty (*yaqīn*):

> *Ḥaqq al-yaqīn* is attained in *fanā'*; it has been symbolized in Ḥallāj's *Kitāb aṭ-ṭawāsīn*, as the way of the moth, which experiences *'ilm al-yaqīn* when it sees the light of the candle, *'ayn al-yaqīn* when it draws

> near and feels its heat, and *ḥaqq al-yaqīn* when it is, finally, burned and consumed by the flame.[9]

"Knowledge of certainty" (*'ilm al-yaqīn*), brings the mystic to the first levels of the partial awareness (*ishrāf-i juz'ī*) of the unveiled entities. The "Vision or eye of certitude" (*'ayn-al yaqīn*) blesses him/her with the advanced level of the partial awareness. In this level of certainty, "the eye of the heart" (*'ayn al-qalb*) is well-prepared to distinguish the unveiled realities. "The reality or truth of certainty"(*ḥaqq al-yaqīn*) is the level of cosmic awareness (*ishrāf-i kullī*). As we can see, in the symbolism used by Ḥallāj, this level of certainty (*ḥaqq al-yaqīn*) shows the characteristic of the stations of annihilation and subsistence (*fanā'* and *baqā'*). The burning of the moth in the light of the candle, in mystical symbolism, resembles annihilation in the Light of the Absolute and the return of the mystic to the Reality of the Light (i.e., subsistence).

Ḥallāj's mystical yearning for the station of *baqā'* (subsistence) is also shown in one verse of his poem including the phrase"*Uqtulūnī*" (kill me). Through this famous ecstatic poem, he expresses his mystical standing over the whole cosmos (i.e., cosmic awareness) and also invites the faithful friends to be his killers, as he declares his passion for mystical annihilation (*fanā'*). In Ḥallāj's words, the apparent passion for death may have addressed the ultimate passion for mystical annihilation (*fanā'*) and not the bodily annihilation. Generally speaking, in order to experience the mystical annihilation, the mystic does not need to be physically annihilated.

> Kill me, O my faithful friends,
> For my death will be my Life.[10]

His pure submission to God and the appearance of the station of *riḍā* (contentment) are present in different parts of his poetry and sayings. Being in the ultimate station of *ḥaqq al-yaqīn* (the real certitude) leads the mystic's wishes and desires towards total concordance and agreement with the Absolute's Will. "*Riḍā*" is expressed in the poem, "*Yā nasim al-riḥ*" (O breeze of wind). The breeze of wind, with its freshness and its novelty, carries the message of yearning for mystical intimacy with the Absolute to the whole of nature, and delivers the fresh seeds of mystical rapture to the prepared lands (i.e., the hearts of the believers).

> "O breeze of wind, go and tell the Fawn
> Watering only gives me thirst
> (Let Him come), this Friend of mine, whose love is in my heart
> And when He wishes, let Him press my cheek when walking!
> His spirit is my spirit, and my spirit His spirit; Let
> Him desire, and I desire, let me desire, He desires!"[11]

The phrase, "watering only gives me thirst," is used to symbolize the advanced level of annihilation and subsistence (i.e., cosmic awareness). The constant motion of water resembles the constant manifestation of the Absolute which brings consistent freshness and purity to the heart of the mystic. The reference to thirst instead of satisfaction, reveals the capability, preparedness and passion of the mystic for the Absolute's manifestations and the return towards Him.

Bāyazīd Basṭāmī

Bāyazīd Basṭāmī (d. 260/874), the well-known Persian mystic, is considered by some scholars to be "the first to speak openly of annihilation of the self in God (*fanā' fi-Allāh*) and subsistence through God (*baqā' bi-Allāh*)".[12]

Like Ḥallāj, his mystical ecstasy has been manifested in famous "*shaṭḥiyāt.*" Annemarie Schimmel provides an explanation of this term.

> It is in the state of absorption that the mystics have sometimes uttered expressions that do not fit into the orthodox views, or even into moderate Sufism. The so-called "*shaṭḥiyāt*" (plural of *shaṭḥ*), like Ḥallāj's *ana al-Ḥaqq* or Bāyazīd's "Glory be to Me! How great is My Majesty"....[13]

Within Bāyazīd's mystical expressions about *fanā'* and *baqā'*, we may recognize the mystical state of "*sukr*" or intoxication. In this state, the eruption of joy is paradoxically mixed with "*ṣaḥw*," sobriety. Although in this state the mystic is intoxicated with the manifestation of the Truth, he is nonetheless aware of the new effusions that are manifesting themselves to him:

> Bāyazīd once uttered the call to prayer and fainted. When he came to his senses he said: it is amazing that a man does not die when uttering the call to prayer.[14]

Bāyazīd expresses the mystical ability to share in the cosmic harmony when the heart receives a series of unveiled manifestations of the Truth. In understanding the cosmic order, the mystic, on his way toward proximity to the Absolute, endeavors to recognize the substantial essences (*dhawāt*) of his environment, and gradually shares in the infinite and meaningful "cosmic order" (*niẓām-i hastī*). Realizing this fact in the deepest layers of his experience at the time of prayer to the only Origin of the whole cosmos, the mystic, in an indescribable joy and astonishment (*ḥayrah*), faints and his ordinary senses transmute and return to the higher level of His Presence.

Despite the seemingly disdainful feature of Bāyazīd's controversial statement, "Glory be to Me! How Great is My Majesty," it shows his experience of *fanā'* and *baqā'* with its strong connection to the mystical station of *faqr* (poverty). In the station of *faqr*, the mystic is genuinely aware of his/her essential need for the Absolute. This awareness of the intense need for the Absolute develops into an intense feeling of contentment (*ghanā'*) regardless of material needs, even if the mystic has the benefit of having them all. The material benefits of this world, for the mystic are not the goal and in their best form only appear as the tools to help him/her in the mystical path. This does not mean that Islamic mystics have not had any material property, but rather that they have freedom of soul from material attachment or worldly benefit. This non-attachment in the mystical view even includes the Divine rewards in the Hereafter. In other words, an advanced mystic seeks the mystical path only for the sake of the Absolute and not in exchange for Heaven. The supreme Heaven for the mystic is the presence of the Absolute. This mystical station reaches its profound levels in the experience of annihilation and subsistence. In the constant experience of mystical annihilation and subsistence (*fanā'* and *baqā'*), the "sanctity" (manifestation of the Absolute), becomes the domain of the experience *and* the whole existence of the mystic who comes from sheer need and poverty and is filled with the infinite richness of the Absolute. The mystic in this profound level, in each experience of annihilation, becomes annihilated from one aspect of his/her "poverty" (*faqr*) and then immediately experiences a profound sense of "contentment and richness" (*ghanā'*) in the subsistence within the Absolute's manifestation. The reality of this relation with the Absolute is the tie between the lover and the Beloved rather than the beggar and the Giver.

The experience of Bāyazīd represents the mystic's awareness of his "absolute poverty" (*faqr-i kāmil*) before the Absolute. The more intense the reality of the mystical poverty in the soul of the mystic, the more substantial is the return as it becomes tantamount to spiritual "richness and contentment" (*ghanā'*). Absorbing the essence of mystical "poverty" (*faqr*) for the mystic is the essence of the most valuable richness. Bāyazīd's phrase, which manifests his rapture in a profound mystical richness, in its inward meaning would be "*Glory be to the Absolute, how rich I become in His Majesty*." In such an intense experience of mystical annihilation and subsistence, the mystic in the bounty of his level of "cosmic awareness" also sees the whole existence of the cosmos and all therein, in the absolute poverty and need of the Absolute. For this very reason the real mystics cannot be seduced by something which is poor and do not feel really content or rich by having an entity or position which is poor in its very essence. This is the understanding of mystical Islam from the Qur'ānic revelation as the first and foremost source of Islamic mysticism:

> O mankind ! You are the poor in your relation to Allāh. And Allāh! He is the Absolute, the Owner of Praise. (Qur'ān, 35:15)

The Prophet Muḥammad, pointed to this kind of awareness of *faqr* (poverty) when he stated "*al-faqru fakhrī*:"[15] my poverty is [the source of] my pride.

Abū Ḥamid al-Ghazālī

Abū Ḥamid al-Ghazālī (d. 504/1111), in his *Mishkāt al-Anwār* "The Niche of Lights," divides the mystic's experience of "Ascension to the heaven of Reality" into two states: "*'irfān'an 'Ilmi-yā"* (state of cognitive gnosis) and "*ḥālan dhawqi-yā*"(state of tasting). He mentions Ḥallāj and Bāyazīd's experience to illustrate the state of tasting.

> The gnostics, after having ascended to the heaven of reality, agree that they see nothing in existence save the One, the Real. Some of them possess this state as a cognitive gnosis. Others, however, attain this through a state of tasting. Plurality is totally banished from them, and they become immersed in sheer singularity. Their rational faculties become so satiated that in this state they are, as it were, stunned. No room remains in them for the remembrance of any other than God, nor the remembrance of themselves. Nothing is with them but God. They become so intoxicated with such an intoxication that the ruling authority of their rational faculties is overthrown. Hence, one of them says, "I am the Real!" another, "Glory be to me, how great is my station!" and still another, "There is nothing in my robe but God![16]

Using another mystical controversial phrase from Ḥallāj as an example, Ghazālī expresses his criticism of the public expression of the mystical experience.

> The speech of lovers in the state of intoxication should be concealed and not spread about. When this intoxication subsides, the ruling authority of rational faculty- which is God's balance in His earth- is given back to them. They come to know that what they experienced was not the reality of unification but that it was similar to unification. It was like the word of the lover during the state of extreme passionate love: I am He whom I love and He whom I love is I![17]

This criticism continues in his discussion of *tawḥīd* (proclamation to the Unity of the Absolute) and *ittiḥād* (mystical unification with the Absolute), when he explains the relationship between the state of tasting, mystical intoxication and the concept of *fanā'* (mystical annihilation):

> When this state [tasting and intoxication] gets the upper hand, it is called "extinction" [*fanā'*] in relation to the one who possesses it. Or rather, it is called "extinction from extinction" [*fanā' al-fanā'*] since the possessor of the state is extinct from himself and from his own extinction. For he is conscious neither of himself in that state, nor of his own unconsciousness of himself. If he were conscious of his own unconsciousness, then he would [still] be conscious of himself. In relation to the one immersed in it this state is called "unification" [*ittiḥād*] according to the language of metaphor, or is called "declaring God's

> unity" [*tawḥīd*] according to the language of reality. And behind these realities there are also mysteries, but it would take too long to delve into them.[18] [some explanations added]

Ghazālī distinguishes between the mystical unification with the Absolute (*ittiḥād*) and the declaration of God's Unity (*tawḥīd*), and stresses that the reality of mystical annihilation is a continuous and dynamic station of proclamation to the "Unity of the Absolute"(*tawḥīd*), in which the mystic sees the manifestations of the One everywhere in the whole cosmos. In other words, he elaborates the fact that the return towards the Absolute in the station of annihilation and subsistence is indeed intuition of the sacred domain of the mystical experience, which is the Absolute's manifestation (sanctity). There is no real unification (*ittiḥād*) with the Absolute and even in the most exalted levels of mystical experience, the Absolute remains Absolute and the individual remains himself/herself. Because of the infinite essence of Reality there is always a new domain of experience for the mystic. In other words, the human being as the noblest citizen of the cosmos (the Absolute's creature par excellence), carries an infinite ability to seek the infinite Reality of the Absolute.

It is worth mentioning that this infinite movement toward the Absolute in Islamic mysticism is understood as the *raison d'etre* of the whole cosmos. The cosmos and all components of nature and the environment as one manifestation of the Absolute, is the Absolute's endowment to mankind to be prudently used as the perfect domain in which mankind must fulfil his/her pre-eternal promise to the Absolute. That promise, is the "perpetual quest for perfection" (*istikmāl*) by seeking the Absolute which is the reality of "return" (*istirjā'*).

> And (remember) when your Lord brought forth from the Children of Adam, from their loins, their seeds, and made them testify of themselves, (saying): Am I not your Lord? They said: Yea, surely. We testify. (That was) lest you should say on the Day of Resurrection: Lo! of this we were unaware. (Qur'ān, 7:172)

Ghazālī, in criticizing the public utterance of mystical annihilation (*fanā'*), seems to point out that the mystical annihilation is the crucial station of the soul's journey from the visible (namely the cosmos, the environment and nature) to the Invisible (the Absolute), i.e., the journey from the manifestations to the Manifest.

The cosmos, the environment and nature in the inner meaning of Ghazālī's words reflect a noble highway and existential domain in which the mystic can experience the return toward the Supreme Absolute.

Rūzbihān Baqlī Shirāzī

The experience of "pre-annihilation" in the words of the mystic Rūzbihān Baqlī Shirāzī (d. 605/1209) leads us to another aspect of Ghazālī's explanation of *tawḥīd* (the Unity of the Absolute) and *ittiḥād* (the unification with the Absolute).

Rūzbihān reflects on the perdurable and unveiling manifestations of the Absolute in the station of pre-annihilation, by comparing these two floating waves of mystical secrets in the ocean of Reality. Through the oceans of mystical intuition in pre-annihilation, the mystic, passes from inherent existence (nature and environment) to the Presence of the Absolute Existence.

> I saw oceans upon oceans, greatness upon greatness,

> fields upon fields, and I nearly was annihilated in the accumulated oceans of pre-eternity. When He realized my inability to bear the weight of the calamities of unity, He abandoned me and left. I returned to where I was.[19]

In Rūzbihān's explanation of "annihilation" the state of *ḥayrah* (mystical astonishment), which is a result of *hayba* (reverence or awe before the Absolute's manifestations), is clearly expressed. The mystic receives the transcendental ability for annihilation and nearness to nobility (*iṣālah*) in his/her cosmic place and, free from the darkness of uncertainty, finds the very real quintessence of his/her mystical presence in His Presence. Using one Qur'ānic verse, Rūzbihān explains his experience of annihilation.

> "Everything is perishing but His Face" (Qur'ān 28:88). That is the station of singleness and annihilation. I remained astonished and was annihilated, and I do not know where I was. Then He approached me until He drew near, until I was hidden and annihilated. God is beyond every fancy indication and expression.[20]

The ocean, as one of the major natural symbols, and the domain of mystical experience, represents the reality of the mystic's experience. Sanctity appears here in the manifestation of the ocean. The ocean is one of the symbolic domains of mystical experience. Although each wave is like the one epiphany of the Absolute, the ocean as a whole reflects the Single Source of sanctity, and points to the reality of *tawḥīd* (the Unity of the Absolute).

Rūzbihān's experience of pre-annihilation, takes place

in the waves of multiplicity. At this stage he has yet to taste universal cosmic awareness (*ishrāf-i kullī*) by connecting all the multiple waves (manifestations of the Absolute) and seeing the unitary reality of the Source (*tawḥīd*). In his experience of the station of annihilation, he achieves the advanced level of cosmic awareness and sees the ocean in its great scale as the ocean itself and not as separate waves (i.e., a journey from multiplicity to Unity). Using the Qur'ānic verse of "every thing is perishing but His Face," in his experience of mystical annihilation, Rūzbihān points to seizing the reality of *tawḥīd* (Unity of the Absolute), which is the reality of the return toward the Absolute. This experience (return) had not taken place during pre-annihilation, as noted by his statement "... He abandoned me and left. I returned to where I was." When he emerges from "partial awareness" to "cosmic awareness," multiplicity of the entities perishes and he meets with the Absolute Unity (His Countenance or symbolically His Face).

Muḥyiddīn Ibn 'Arabī

The mystical stations (*maqāmāt*) of annihilation and subsistence (*fanā'* and *baqā'*) are intertwined. As we have mentioned previously, the advanced nature of experience in mystical annihilation elevates the different levels of the mystic's "partial awareness" to "cosmic awareness." The grand master of Islamic mysticism, Ibn 'Arabī (d. 638/1240), reminds us of the interconnection between mystical annihilation and subsistence:

> Subsistence is your relationship with the Real ... But annihilation is your relationship with the engendered

> universe, since you say, "I have been annihilated from such and such," your relationship to the Real is higher. Hence subsistence is a higher relationship, since the two are interrelated states [stations]. None subsists in this path except him who is annihilated, and none is annihilated except him who subsists.[21] [explanation added]

Here we should mention two groups of Qur'ānic verses which correlate with this approach to mystical annihilation and subsistence (*fanā'* and *baqā'*). The first group consists of several Qur'ānic verses in which the Absolute encourages and invites mankind to observe and reflect upon different parts of the cosmos, nature, environment, and the delicate essence of their creation. These Qur'ānic verses are related to the concept of "*sayr*"(in which travel and observation are done in order to see the "signs [*ayat*] of the Absolute" [cosmos, nature and environment]). The reactions of and the spiritual outcome received by different groups of believers (such as "*mu'minīn*" [29:44] "group of believers," "*mu'qinīn*," "men of certainty" and "*ulu'l al-bāb*"," "men of intellect, reason and reflection") in the process of observing these signs are not equal. In this group of Qur'ānic verses, the different components of creation have been named as signs for different groups of people. Each, with their approach to these signs, has access to a different dimension, level and depth of understanding as well as awareness. Here are some examples of this category of Qur'ānic verses:

> Say (O Muḥammad): Travel in the land and see how He originated creation, then He brings forth the later growth. Lo! Allāh is able to do all things (29:20).

He is Who sends down water from the sky, whence you have drink, and whence are trees on which you send your beasts to pasture. Therewith He causes crops to grow for you, and the olive and the date palm and grapes and all kinds of fruit. Lo! herein is indeed a portent for people who reflect (16:10-11).

Behold! In the creation of the heavens and the earth and the alternation of night and day there are indeed signs for men of understanding (3:190).

The second group of Qur'ānic verses regarding the creation of the cosmos and its entities are related to the concept of *sulūk* (mystical journey). In this group of verses the main focus is on the unitary essence of the cosmos and the concept of return. These verses provide the mystics with different levels of cosmic awareness (*ishrāf-i kullī*) and *tawḥīd* (Unity of the Absolute). Some of these verses address the unitary essence of a "thing" (as the resemblance of the whole cosmos) through its immediate creation by the "one resolution of the Absolute" (*irādat al-Ḥaqq*). The two most prominent verses of this kind are the following:

And Our word unto a thing, when We intend it, is only that We say unto it: Be! and it is (16:40).

And Our commandment is but a single Word, as the twinkling of an eye (54:50).

The whole cosmos, for the mystic is the product of one resolution of the Absolute which represents itself here as one Command (single Word). This single Word which brings the whole cosmos, nature and environment into existence, as the Source of all goodly Words [14:24-25], connects the essence of the whole cosmos (as a goodly tree) to the Lote-tree (*Sidratu'l-Muntahā*) [53:14] in the garden of Heaven [53:15]. The mystic connects him/herself to that ultimate Tree by seeing the whole cosmos as a goodly tree extended up to the Heaven (as constant manifestations) of the Absolute Reality. Therefore, the "horizontal voyage to and observation in the cosmos, nature and the environment" (*sayr*), for the mystic, becomes the "vertical journey to the eternal garden of the Absolute's manifestation" (*sulūk*), and this is the reality of return.

Jalāl al-Dīn Rūmī

The concept of cosmological connectedness with the Real reveals itself in the mystical experiences of the Islamic masters. In the higher level of these experiences, the mystic, from behind the series of falsified veils, is able to see the "real returning" of the whole cosmos, at each instance, towards the Real. The human being, as the viceregent of the Absolute on earth, who thereby carries His trusteeship, is perpetually seeking his/her true place in creation. Using different parts of nature to describe the return towards the Absolute, the 13th century Persian Sufi master, Rūmī (d.672/1273) in his opening chapter of *Mathnawī*, writes:

> I died from inanimate and became animate
> I died from animate and became an animal,
> I died from animality and became a human.
> Why should I be afraid, When have I become less
> by dying?
> [At] the next move I shall die from human,

That I may soar and lift up my head amongst the
angels;
[But] I must escape even from angel[-hood]
"*All things vanish except His Face*"
Once more I shall be sacrificed and die from angel
[-hood]:
I shall become that which enters not into the imagination
Then I shall become non-existence: non-existence
saith to me, (in tones loud) as an organ,
"*Verily, unto Him we are returning*".'[22]

One must not misunderstand Rūmī's words as a theory of evolution or reincarnation. For Rūmī, nature and the environment are the prepared bounty of the Absolute, in which the human being must dwell and then transcend in search of his/her real place in the cosmos (by *returning* to the Absolute). His continuous mention of the expression "I died" (*mordam*) is meant to encourage us to meaningfully ascend to the higher realms of self-realization and again and again (through constant re-creation or *khalq-i mudām*) to the more elevated stages of the mystical journey with each new theophany of the Absolute. In other words, no part of the cosmos is a final station in our existence, but nature and the environment are a bridge aiding in the progression of man's soul toward the perpetual perfection (*istikmāl*). A cause of the abuse and misuse of nature and the environment is the equivocal position that these represent the final goal for man. By borrowing from the primary Source Book of the mystical *tradition*, i.e. the Qur'ān, Rūmī elaborates on the eternal presence of the Source of *sanctity* (the Absolute), and accentuates the *experi-*

ence of return, endowing the Islamic mystic with the essence of humanity. Non-existence (*'adam*) in fact becomes the *sine qua non* of true existence (*hastī*). Therefore, for Rūmī *'adam* alludes to the station of mystical annihilation (*fanā'*) which incessantly embraces subsistence (*baqā'*). *Istirjā'* (seeking perpetual return towards the Absolute) occurs in the domain of sanctity (the eternal presence of the Absolute) as the only domain of the mystical experience. *Fanā'* and *baqā'* are the prominent presences of the experience of "return."

The bounty of the "unveiling the essences"(*Kashf al-dhawāt*) of the cosmos, is achieved through the experiences of *fanā'* and *baqā'*. Rūmī refers to the reciprocal consciousness of existence in the presence of the Absolute.

> This earth has the mark of God's clemency (*ḥilm*)
> In that it got filth and gave flowers as the produce[23]

The universal confession of the whole being is expressed in several Qur'ānic verses such as verse 41 from chapter 24:

> Seest thou not that it is Allāh Whose praises all beings in the heavens and on earth do celebrate, and the birds (of the air) with wings outspread? each one knows its own (mode of) prayer and praise. And Allāh knows well all that they do.

3. A Stratospheric Example: Light

In Islamic mystical texts, the cosmic effusions of "light" are among the most popular symbols. Using different Qur'ānic verses, the mystical interpretations of light are expounded around the images of "things as they really are" (levels of certainty-*yaqīn*), as opposed to the shadows of the veils (*ḥijāb*-uncertainty) in the darkness (*ẓulmah*). The 11th century Sufi master al-Qushayrī in his famous "Treatise of Qushayriyah,"(*risālah al-Qushayriyah*) utilizes this symbol in his mystical experience of annihilation or *fanā'*. In the constant motion towards intimacy with the Absolute, the mystic passes through the states of attendance (*al-muhaḍara*) and unveiling (*al-mukāshafa*), and finally comes to witnessing (*al-mushāhada*). In this state, the mystic leaves behind all the multiplicities which have risen from the darkness and the glimmering of faint lights and ultimately reaches the Light. The symbolic poetry which is cited in his treatise "Morning's Light" exemplifies the light of *tawḥīd* which embraces all the shimmerings of the stars. The mystic is guided by each cup of Unity's Light and becomes emancipated from all perplexities of multifarious and un-trustful lights.

> When morning appears
> its light extinguishes
> the light of the lights
> of the stars.
> It gives people a swallow
> from a cup
> that were they suffering from a blazing fire
> one gulp would put it out immediately.[24]

In one of the Qur'ānic examples which is emphasized by different Sufi masters in their mystical interpretations of the Qur'ān, the Absolute is symbolized by the "Light of the heavens and the earth." Using niche, lamp, star and olive tree, the illumination of this Light is described in a unique allegory:

> Allāh is the Light of the heavens and the earth. The parable of His Light is as if there were a Niche and within it a Lamp: The Lamp enclosed in Glass: The glass as it were a brilliant star: lit from a blessed Tree, an Olive, neither of the East nor of the West, Whose oil is well-nigh luminous, though fire scarce touched it: Light upon Light! Allāh doth guide whom He will to His Light Allāh doth set forth parables for men and Allāh doth know all things. (chapter of Light, verse 35)

Rūmī says:

> Man's original food is the Light of God
> Animal food is improper (*nāsezāst*) for him.[25]

4. Mystical Islam and the Concept of Constant Re-creation (*Khalq-i Mudām*)

In the view of Islamic mysticism, nature, the environment, and the organic whole of existence, in its most minute detail, become completely new at each instance. This idea stems from the interpretation of some Qur'ānic verses.

> Were We then weary with the first creation, that they should be in confused doubt about a new creation? (50:15)

Another Qur'ānic example related to this concept is found in chapter 55 verse 29:

> Of Him seeks (its need) every creature in the heavens and on earth: every day in (new) splendor doth

He (shine).

In the mystical understanding of the new creation, existence at each moment embraces a new Divine effusion (*tajallī*). Through this everlasting renewal, the entire creation is extinguished in a moment and revived and refreshed at the very next instance. In this sense, concepts of annihilation and subsistence (*fanā'* and *baqā'*) enter a cosmic level. With each new manifestation of the Truth, the whole cosmos, nature and the environment experiences a totally new opportunity to breathe and flourish again. This concept is elaborated upon by Ibn 'Arabī:

> At root the substance of the cosmos is one. It never changes from its reality... The Real bring similars (*amthāl*) into existence perpetually (*'ala'l-dawām*) since He is the Creator perpetually, while the possible things in the state of their nonexistence possess the preparedness to receive existence. No non-existence ever overcomes the cosmos in respect of its substance, nor does any form ever remain for two instants. Creation never ceases, while the entities are receivers, which take off and put on [existence]. So in every instant (*nafas*) the cosmos in respect of its form undergoes a new creation in which there is no repetition".[26]

Referring to the Qur'ānic verse (50:15) about new creation, he explains the absurdity of any resemblance of the two moments:

> The cosmos is never fixed in a single state for a moment, since God is Ever-creating constantly.

> Were the cosmos to remain in a single state for two moments, it would be described by independence from God. But people are "in confusion as to a new creation."[27]

Explaining the second Qur'ānic verse (55:29), Ibn 'Arabī interprets *yawm* (day) as "a moment" in this verse:

> He is 'each day upon some task.' The day is the indivisible moment, while the task is that God causes to occur within it. Days are many; some are long some are short. The smallest of them is the indivisible moment, in respect of which came the verse... God named the indivisible moment a 'day' because a 'task' is made to occur within it. So it is the shortest and the most minute of days.[28]

5. Mullā Ṣadrā and the "Transubstantial Motion" (*ḥarakat al-jawharia*)

The centrality of the perpetual re-creation intertwined with the cosmic annihilation and subsistence, and the ceaseless relationship of the entire existence with the Real leads us to the notion of living cosmos. Because all of creation is encompassed within constant manifestations of the Truth, creation will never experience non-existence. Through the continuous currents of the disclosure of the Real, which are the Absolute's emanation (*fayḍ*), the cosmos constantly experiences another living wave of its motion toward Eternity.

The prominent Persian philosopher and mystic, Ṣadrā al-Dīn Shīrāzī (Mullā Ṣadrā, d. 1050/1640) named this essential tendency of existence to a constant and conscious motion toward Eternity, "transubstantial motion" (*ḥarakat al-jawharia*). The word *jawhar* (substance) in Mullā Ṣadrā's expression indicates that this essential and fundamental *harakah* (motion) is the primordial necessity of each substance and essence in the whole cosmos. In its constant flourishing, re-creation and renewal, the entire cosmos, like a keen river, moves and migrates from the very previous moment to the next. This cosmic experience includes not only each substance (*jawhar*), but also every occurrence or accident (*'araḍ*). The transubstantial motion of the *jawāhir* (substances) encompasses also the *a'rāḍ* (accidents), and both participate in the invigorating waves of this experience.[29]

As Rūmī says:

The word is like the nest, and the meaning is the
bird: the body is the river-bed, and the spirit is
the rolling water.
It is moving and you say it is standing: it is running,
and you say it is keeping still.
If you see not the movement of the water through
the clods of earth–(yet it is moving): what are
the sticks and straws (ever appearing) anew on it?
Your sticks and straws are the forms (ideas) of
thought, as it rolls, is not without sticks and
straws, (some) pleasing and (some) unsightly.
The husks on the surface of this rolling water have
sped along from the fruits of the Invisible Garden.
Seek the kernel of the husks (not on the water, but)
in the Garden, because the water comes from
the Garden into the river-bed.

> If you see not the flow of the Water of Life, look at this movement of weeds in the stream.
> When the water begins to pass by in the fuller volume, the husks, (which are) the ideas, pass along it more quickly.
> When this stream has become extremely rapid in its flow, no care lingers in the minds of gnostics. [30]

The mystic sees the motion of the whole cosmos as it provides us with the new fruits of intimacy with the Absolute in the path of perfection and return. In the mystical view of transubstantial motion, the cosmos rises to a new phase of proximity and elevation with each new manifestation of the Absolute.

> This world and that world are for ever giving birth
> Every cause is a mother, the effect is born (from it as) a child.[31]

6. Islamic Cosmic Strata

In the general views of the Islamic cosmic strata which are extensively described by the mystics, the terrestrial world, as one of the five stages of being, is a reflection of the Absolute. "*Hahūt*," or the realm of the Divine Essence, "*lāhūt*," or the realm of Divine Attributes, "*jabarūt*," or the angelic realm, "*malakūt*," or the realm of elusive epiphanies, are preceded by the state of "*nāsūt*" as the physical domain. Discussion of "*nāsūt*," as the terrestrial world with mankind as its noblest creature, leads us to the key concept of the "perfect human being" (*insān al-kāmil*), as the sixth stage.[32] In the Islamic belief, the Prophet of Islam is the most exalted example of the perfect human being.

7. Concept of Universal/Perfect Human Being (*insān al-kāmil*) and its Place in Islamic Cosmology

In view of Islamic mysticism, *insān al-kāmil* is the ultimate goal of God's creation. As the Prophetic tradition explains, the heart of the universal human being corresponds to the Divine Throne (*'arsh*). In the mystical view of Islam, this coherence is an organic correspondence.

In his masterpiece, *Fuṣūṣ al-Ḥikam*, Master Magnus Ibn 'Arabī describes the status of the perfect human being:

> It is through him that God looks at His creatures and dispenses His Mercy upon them; for he is the adventitious man, and yet he has no beginning; he is ephemeral and yet he is everlastingly eternal. He is also the Word which divides and unites. The word subsists in virtue of his existence. He is to the world what the setting of a seal is to the seal: that is to say the place where the imprint is engraved, the symbol with which the king seals his treasures. This is why he has been called *Khalifa* [lieutenant, vicar, deputy]:for through him God preserves His creation, as the seal preserve the treasure. As long as the king's seal remains unbroken, no one would dare to open his treasures without his permission. Thus Man has been charged to guard the kingdom, and the world will be preserved for as long as the Perfect Man subsists therein.[33]

For the Islamic mystic who is endowed with the ultimate passion and rapture of approaching the station of the universal human being, each sincere deed and intention towards absolute submission before the Absolute, will lead him/her to the unique meaning of *Islam* (peace and total submission to God). As a result, the mystic will be guided towards the boundless inward and outward peace with the entire cosmos.

Referring to the above mentioned Prophetic tradition (*hadith*) the 14th century Sufi master, Ala'ad-Dawla Simnānī expresses the association of the station of annihilation (*fanā'*) with the stage of the perfect human being (*insān al-kāmil*).

> I don't know why I am, or who I am, or how I am
> All I know is I am carrying the throne of God's law.[34]

In the infinite dimensions of peace, pure submission and mystical certainty (*yaqīn*), for the mystic, who lives in the total presence of the Absolute, every minute part of nature and the environment is the magnificent realm of His presence. The true believer sees the environment as God's bounty, and as His viceregent in constant harmony with the cosmos, respects and cares for the environment like a tireless and compassionate gardener and guardian.

Referring to the Qur'ān (4:126), Rūmī reminds us that existence as a whole is enveloped in the presence of the Absolute. A mystic lives in and experiences His eternal presence which is the realm of His *sanctity*.

> Every thing (*jomleh*) is encompassed by the Truth
> None of His manifestations confutes another.[35]

Man with his free will participates in the Supreme Resolution (*irādat al-Ḥaqq*) in order to judiciously use nature and the environment as the Absolute's bounty. In this view, any immoderate use of nature is recognized as a revolt against the Supreme Law. Receiving and realizing His manifestations (*tajalliyāt*) from each part of the environment and cosmos, a true mystic intermeshes every one of his/her worldly acts and deeds with his/her eternal afterlife. Therefore, in Islamic mysticism, each instance of this "earthly life" (*dunyā*), in reality, embraces the "hereafter" (*ākhirah*) and the mystic has the proper faculty to experience the real resurrection which occurs in every moment of his/her mundane life. In a life founded on proximity to God, responsible use of nature and the environment as His sacred signs facilitates this sacred journey of the believer toward the Real Beloved.

> From there (*zān ṭaraf*), trailing the skirt (of glory), it [water] evokes Lessons concerning the purifications (*ṭahārāt*) of [their] environment (*muḥīṭ*).[36]

The perennial passion of the mystic, through the Absolute's manifestations in the cosmos, nature and the environment, leads him/her to be a witness to the Divine's Principles, and to recognize the real order and *true nature of nature* (*dhāt al-ṭabi'ah*). Rūmī tells us that the seemingly unvoiced and paralyzed (*afsordeh*) world will reveal its words to the prodigies who are able to see the constant "motion of the world"(*jonbesh-i jesm-i jahān*) under the radiant sun of resurrection (*khorshīd-i ḥashr*). Every particle of the cosmos proclaims:

> We have hearing (*sami'īm*) and sight (*baṣirīm*), and are happy (*khoshīm*).
> [Although] with you, the uninitiated, we are mute.[37]

Acquaintance with the "substances" (*jawāhir*) in the cosmos, nature and environment, will guide the mystic to reacquaint his/her "essentia" with the objective realization of a living notion. Passing through "occurrences" (*a'rāḍ*) towards the essences (*dhawāt*) in nature and the environment, the mystic takes a journey from the colored multiplicities towards intuition in the presence of the Absolute Existence. Existence in the cosmos and nature manifests itself as a mirror, which projects to the mystic, the *sanctity*, i.e., the eternal presence of the Absolute. This is another aspect of mystical capability through preparation of the crucial stations of *fanā'* and *baqā'*. Islamic mystical *tradition* elaborates on the enduring presence of the *sanctity* through which a mystic *experiences* the unremitting joy of the *return* towards the Absolute.

The universal human being is the *par excellence* of the eternal journey of the whole cosmos in the path of return.

> The light of the sun heard [the call] *irja'ī* (return)
> [And] came back in haste to its Source.[38]

8. Examples from the Natural and Environmental Symbols and Allegories in Islamic Mysticism

In the works of Islamic masters, we are witness to the symbolic and allegorical analysis of the numerous natural and environmental components. Making use of Qur'ānic verses, Islamic mystics have employed *water*, *wind*, *cloud*, *rain* and *ocean* as symbols and allegories to convey several mystical themes.

One of the Qur'ānic verses describes the revival of the dead land with the help of the wind, clouds and rain. This event is symbolic of God's mercy, and an allegory for raising people from the dead. In the verse which follows, "clean land" (*al-balad al-ṭayyib*), symbolizes the heart of a believer who is capable of growing and yielding fruit through deeds of righteousness under God's effusions and bounty. It is juxtaposed to the heart of the disbeliever, which will bear no fruit.

> It is He Who sendeth the winds like heralds of glad tidings, going before His Mercy: when they have carried the heavy-laden clouds. We drive them to a land that is dead, make rain to descend thereon, and produce every kind of harvest therewith: thus shall we raise up the dead: perchance ye may remember.
>
> From the land that is clean and good, by the Will of its cherisher, springs up produce, (rich) after its kind: But from the land that is bad, springs up nothing but that which is scanty, thus do we explain the signs by various (symbols) to those who are grateful. (Qur'ān, 7:57, 58)

Using another Qur'ānic verse, Annemarie Schimmel describes the use of rain and ocean as symbolism for the Prophet of Islam:

> The image of the ocean for God (or, in poetry, for love, which may even be an 'ocean of fire') is generally valid, but the Prophet too has been called an ocean in which the Qur'ān constitutes the precious pearl. More frequently, however, is the combination of the Prophet with the rain.
>
> For rain was sent down to quicken the dead earth

> (Sūrah, 41:39), and it is still called *raḥmat*, 'mercy' in some areas of the Turkish and Persian world. Thus it was easy to find cross-relation between the 'rain of mercy' and him who is called in the Qur'ān *raḥmat li' l-'ālamīn*, 'mercy for the worlds' (Sūrah, 21:107). Muḥammad himself, as Abu Hafs Omar as-Suhrawardi tells in his *'Awārif al-Ma'ārif* was fond of the precious rain and used to turn to the rain to accept blessing from it and said, "one that was still recently near his Lord."[39]

The Prophet Muḥammad, who is considered by Muslims to have brought the most complete message of God and who himself is believed to be the most exalted "*uswatun ḥasanah*" (the best model of perfection), exhorts mystics to name him with delicate and elegant symbols.

> The Sindhi mystical poet, Shāh 'abdul Laṭif (d. 1752), devoted his *Sur Sarang* to him, ingeniously blending the description of the parched land that longs for rain with the hope for the arrival of the beloved Prophet, who appears as the rain-cloud that stretches from Istanbul to Delhi and even further. A century later, Mirzā Ghālib in Delhi (d.1869) composed a Persian *mathnavī* about 'The Pearl-carrying Cloud', i.e. the Prophet, and towards the end of nineteenth century Muḥsin Kākorawī (d. 1905) sang his famous Urdu ode in honour of the Prophet, skillfully blending the theme of the cloud and the 'rain of mercy' with time-honoured indigenous Indian rain poetry.[40]

Mystics have also used the annihilation and subsistence of the rain in the ocean to symbolize the infinite and profound return of the whole cosmos to the One Substantial Source.

> ... Rain has yet another aspect to it. It comes from the ocean, rises, evaporating, to the sky, condenses again in the clouds and returns finally to the ocean to be united with its original source or else, as was popularly thought, to become a pearl enriched by a pure oyster.[41]

In their interpretations of the Qur'ān, the mystics have reflected upon the concept of the intelligent cosmos and environment. Not only does all of creation lie within the Absolute's Presence, but it is also aware of this presence. In one of the Qur'ānic examples, God compares the hardened hearts of one group of non believers to rocks; blaming their hearts for being more non-reflexive and hardened than rocks (*ashaddū qaswah*). Three categories of rocks are described, each representing a different level of awareness of His Presence; a Presence which is entrusted among these most seemingly silent and unconscious parts of nature.

> Thenceforth were your hearts hardened: they became like a rock and even worse in hardness. For among rocks there are some from which rivers gush forth; others there are, which when split asunder, send forth water: and others which sink for fear of Allāh, and Allāh is not unmindful of what ye do. (Qur'ān, 2:74)

Rūmī with his understanding of the human being's infinite ability as the noblest creature, referred to him/her as both "microcosm" and "macrocosm."

Therefore in form thou art the microcosm (*'ālam-i asghar*)
Therefore, in reality thou art the macrocosm (*'ālam-i akbar*).[42]

Annihilation and subsistence are two of the most eminent stations in which the mystic can experience the spiritual encounter with his/her infinite faculties by both being macrocosm and microcosm. These two higher stations place the mystic in the real order of things, bringing him/her closer to the real place of the human being in the cosmos.

One significance of being a macrocosm is the discovery of the meaningful aim of the whole cosmos, nature and the environment. An Islamic mystic, by following the only True Goal, becomes a torchbearer for those in the never-ending journey of existence toward the Absolute Existence. Rūmī says in his *Mathnawī*:

My falcon-drum is the call, *irja'ī* (return)
God is my witness (*guwāh*) in spite of adversary (*mudda'ī*).[43]

Chapter II

The Methodology

In this chapter, I clarify the affinities of each dimension of the triangle (sanctity, tradition and experience) with the three concepts of "cosmos, nature and environment" as well as how they relate to each other. To narrow the field of observation and avoid generalization, I use the same framework of experience, i.e., "mystical annihilation and subsistence" (*fanā'* and *baqā'*) in Islamic mysticism. I discuss the dimension of "*tradition*" through a critique of Annemarie Schimmel's discussion of *wujūd* (existence); the dimension of "*experience*" through a review of Toshihiko Izutsu's approach to the experience of *fanā'* (mystical annihilation); and the dimension of "*sanctity*" through Emile Durkheim's understanding of the "sacred," as the dominant view of contemporary western scholars. My critique of some specific views of these scholars is in no way meant to undermine their contributions in their own fields. Throughout the discussion, the concept of "return" as the examiner of the triangle will be addressed. The essentiality of this concept in Islamic mysticism allows us to utilize it as the examiner of the correct function of the suggested triangle.

In the second section, I provide some examples from Islamic mystics to address the role of "return" in relation to "man and cosmos."

This will all be done with concentration on the concepts of cosmos, nature, and environment in Islamic mysticism. By understanding the function and affinities of the three dimensions of the suggested triangle and having the centrality of the concept of "return" in mind, we can effectively approach the main concepts in Islamic mysticism.

1. Concept of "*return*" (*istirjā'*) in Islamic Mysticism and its Implications for Cosmos, Nature and Environment

Tradition

When we are facing a term rooted in the very embodiment of the Islamic mystical tradition, it is not simply enough to approach it etymologically, but rather one must allow the organic whole of the tradition to identify the term itself. This is specially so when the term is part of a doctrinal concern in this tradition. In such a case its attachment to the mystical and even philosophical observations should be considered. One such term is *wujūd*, which provides us with both views in Islamic philosophy and mysticism. Before trying to decipher a relevant example from the Islamic mystical tradition, I quote an explanation of the term used to approach the concept of *fanā'*.

A prominent scholar of Islamic mysticism, Annemarie Schimmel writes,

> *Fanā'* is, in the beginning, an ethical concept: man becomes annihilated and takes on God's attributes—it

> is the place of the alleged hadith *takhallaqū bi-akhlaq Allāh*—qualify yourself with the qualities of God, i.e., through constant mental struggle exchange your own base qualities for the praiseworthy qualities by which God described Himself in the Koranic revelation. The next stage is the annihilation in vision, when the soul is surrounded by the primordial light of God. The third and final stage, then, is "annihilation from one's vision of annihilation," in which one is immersed in the *wujūd*, the "existence" of God or, rather, the "finding" of God. For the word *wujūd* which is usually translated as "existence," means, originally, the "being found"—*and that is what the mystic experiences.*[44] [emphasis added]

The interpretations of the term—*wujūd*—have a long history of discussions and arguments in both Islamic philosophy and mystical tradition. Islamic philosophers and mystics have categorized and classified the varieties and types of this concept.[45] In order to get a sense of the term *wujūd*, I would point to a concrete characteristic of the concept explained by Islamic philosophers. One of the attributes of this term is said to be"*badihi'un mu'arrif'un bidhāti-hi,*"[46] "the most obvious [concept] which defines itself by its [very] essence [substance]." In the first interpretations around the term *wujūd* and its "self-explanatory/self-referential clarity" (*bidāha*), Islamic philosophers have argued that in order to come up with a "defined concept" (*mu'arraf*), the "definer" (*mu'arrif*) has to be clearer (*ajlā*) and more obvious (*aẓhar*) than the "defined concept" (*mu'arraf*).[47] Then, basing themselves on this rule for a proper definition, they have concluded that "there is no definer for the term *wujūd*"[48] (*lā mu'arrif lil-wujūd*). In order to break down the complication of the philosophical aspects of the argument, we should use some simple examples. For example when one says: "he *is*," "I *am*," "that *is*," "you *are*" or "they *are*," there are no clearer or more obvious concepts out there to define the reality behind such words as "is," "am,"and "are." Thus, in the initial approach to *wujūd*, in Islamic philosophical tradition, the *bidāha* of this concept provides us with a common attribute for different subjects of the propositions. This common attribute is the fact that all of them *exist*.

The above mentioned attribute of *wujūd*, namely *bidāha* (self-explanatory/self-referential clarity), turns into another realm when it comes to the Islamic mystical tradition. Here, *wujūd* takes on a particular *cosmic* understanding.

In the eyes of Islamic mystics, "cosmos and all which exists therein" *is* one spark of the manifestation of the Real. "The reality of the existence" (*haqīqat al-wujūd*) of the cosmos springs from the Reality of "Existence" (*Wujūd*). Therefore, the *bidāha* (self-explanatory/self-referential clarity) of *wujūd* displays itself in the whole cosmos. For the mystic, this *bidāha*, testifies that the self-disclosure of the only Real Manifest, has been projected in the most perfect clarity. In other words, in the whole cosmos you see nothing save the Existence (*Wujūd*) of the One. This most perfect clarity (as the feature of *bidāha*), for the mystic, extends to the degree that he/she sees the whole cosmos as the presence of the Manifest. In the constant "annihilation and subsistence" (*fanā'* and *baqā'*) of the whole cosmos, the Light of the Manifest brings the entire cosmos from sheer darkness of non-existence (*'adam*) to existence (*wujūd*). The grand master of Islamic mysticism, Ibn 'Arabī declares,

> The cosmos is not identical with the Real; it is only what becomes manifest within the Real *Wujūd*.[49]

He also says,

> He is *wujūd*, nothing else. That which He calls the "cosmos" is the name Manifest, and it is His face.[50]

The Manifest (*Ẓāhir*) is one of the Qur'ānic names of the Absolute (57:3). It is worth mentioning that this name also means "Evident," and from this comes the mystical "clarity" (*bidāha*) of *wujūd* and cosmos, because, for the mystic the whole cosmos is "evidently" nothing but a manifestation of the Absolute. Ibn 'Arabī declares,

> The cosmos stays upon its root in nonexistence, but it has a ruling property in what becomes manifest in the *wujūd* of the Real. So there is nothing there but the Real-un-differentiated and differentiated.[51]

We might state that Ibn 'Arabī, with the term "undifferentiated," addresses the mystical view of cosmos as one undifferentiated manifestation of the Absolute (cosmos as a whole), and with "differentiated," he refers to the usual view of the cosmos, i.e., seeing it as "the components of nature and environment."

The constant motion of the cosmos from non-existence to existence is indeed the reality of *return* to the Absolute. In the eyes of Islamic mystics, the yearning for return lies in the very essence (*dhāt*) of the cosmos. Thus, without return, there is no existence. Therefore, every aspect of the Islamic mystical tradition is intermeshed with the essence of return to the level that we might say is the *tradition of return towards the Absolute*.

Thus, with all respect to the late Professor Schimmel's effort, we should remark that in the mystic's experience in the station of annihilation (*fanā'*), *wujūd* as the Self disclosure of the Absolute need *not to be found and defined*, but returns toward Him. In other words, for the mystic, there is nothing in the whole cosmos save the presence of the Absolute. The "manifestation of the Absolute's Presence" (Absolute *Wujūd*), provides mankind with the *wujūd* (existence) which, for the Islamic mystic, is the only domain of experience. In his/her experience of the cosmic awareness (*ishrāf-i kullī*), especially in the stations of *fanā'* and *baqā'*, the mystic has the ultimate capability to unveil the disclosures of the Absolute. Manifestations become apparent and clear to him/her and envelop the reality of the mystic, that is, the whole *wujūd* which is aware of the Absolute's Presence, and in constant motion, *returns* to the Absolute. The mystic, in the stations of *fanā'* and *baqā'* becomes the torchbearer of the cosmic return towards the Absolute.

Sanctity

Sanctity (the manifestation of the Absolute), is both the "*domain of mystical experience*" and the whole existence of the mystic. Cosmos is the manifestation of the Absolute (sanctity), which represents His sacred presence. The mystic, in the experience of annihilation and subsistence and in the ultimate awareness of this sanctity, views the whole cosmos as one manifestation of the Absolute and reaches the profound awareness of *tawḥīd* (Unity of the Absolute).

The famous sociologist Emile Durkheim (1857-1917), has defined the "sacred" as "*something added to and above the real.*"[52] This approach to the "sacred" is almost a dominant view among contemporary western scholars.

Through the experience of *fanā'* and *baqā'*, the mystic, in the unremitting renewal of the whole cosmos, sees this whole as a single manifestation of the Absolute which carries a *single sacred consciousness.* This sacred consciousness conveys a sacred yearning which is nothing but the aspiration of *return* towards the Absolute. In the constant annihilation and subsistence of the *undivided cosmos* (cosmos as a whole), the consciousness of return, animates the whole cosmos with the essence of sacredness. In this understanding of the sacred, the sacred (cosmos), is not "added to" or "above" the real, but *is* a single disclosure or manifestation of the Real. To make this view clearer, I will refer to the mystical station of *jam'* (collectedness) which overlaps *with* the station of mystical annihilation and subsistence (*fanā'* and *baqā'*).

Reaching the station of *jam'* is one of the most challenging and arduous tasks along the mystical path. Mystics usually experience *jam'* at the level of a short "state" (*ḥāl*) and fail to reach it in a long "station" (*maqām*). *Jam'* is the gathering of all of the mystic's senses and thoughts in one single consciousness when he/she embraces the manifestation of the Absolute. In other words, *jam'* is the collectedness of the mystic's "being" in one single consciousness through which he/she encounters the single manifestation of the Absolute. This collectedness of the mystic's being (*jam'*) has its own levels of profoundness. In the experience of mystical annihilation and subsistence (*fanā'* and *baqā'*), the mystic is in the perfect/comprehensive awareness of the interconnectedness of his/her whole "being," and sees the whole cosmos as one collected being.

In the cosmic view of this station (*jam'*), the essences of the beings in the cosmos are enveloped by one collective conscious being, which denounces any type of divisions and separation. Separation and division (*farq* or *tafrīq*) are the opposite of *jam'*. One of the major concerns of mystics in the domain of experience is to exist perpetually in the station of *jam'*. Tasting mystical annihiltion and subsistence is impossible without experiencing this overlapping station (i.e., *jam'*).

In other words, *jam'* is one of the essential requirements for the mystic to reach the stations of annihilation and subsistence. When a mystic reaches these stations, in the advanced awareness of the sacred surrounding of the Absolute's Presence, he/she sees the annihilation and subsistence of the cosmos as *a whole*. The mystic sees this as the proclamation of the whole cosmos to the Unity (*tawḥīd*) of the Absolute, which is the reality of return. The sanctity becomes the essence of the whole being and the domain of experience and *not* an extra concept which is "added to or above the real."

Experience

According to the prominent Japanese scholar of Islamic mysticism, the late Professor Toshihiko Izutsu,

> *Fanā'* is certainly a human experience. It is man who actually experiences it. *But it is not solely a human experience. For when he does experience it, he is no longer himself.* In this sense, man is not the subject of experience. The subject is rather metaphysical reality itself. In

> other words, the human experience of *fanā'* is itself the self actualization of reality...[53] [emphasis added]

Fanā' and *baqā'* are not experiences that discard the "concept of being human," but rather that enrich the everlasting tendencies toward the enrichment of this concept. In experiencing each mystical station, the mystic becomes a more transcended "human being" in the path of perpetual perfection as viceregent of the Absolute (*khalifatu'llāh*). This constant movement towards perfection provides the seekers with the opportunity to be the *noblest citizens of the cosmos* (*ashraf al-makhlūqāt*). In this pathway towards perfection, man is in the ideal position to ascertain the inner connectedness with the very essence of the sacred "manifestations of the Absolute" (sanctity), and harmony with the cosmos.

In Islam, as a primordial religion, the pivotal concept of *Unity* (*tawḥīd*) penetrates each dimension of art, science, and theology, as well as philosophy and mysticism. In the crucial stations of annihilation and subsistence the mystic sees the new epiphanies of the Absolute as the manifestations of this Unity. *Tawḥīd* (the Unity of the Absolute) represents the return of the whole cosmos. The cosmos carries the creed (*shahādah*) of the Unity of the Absolute. This creed in mystical reality is the constant remembrance (*dhikr-i mudām*) of the One by the citizens of the cosmos. The content and beauty of this creed is not unveiled to everyone, but the mystic in the splendid stations of *fanā'* and *baqā'* has the proper faculty to realize this cosmic declaration.

> "The seven heavens and the earth, and all beings therein, declare His glory: There is not a thing but celebrates His praise; and yet ye understand not how

> to declare His glory! Verily He is Oft-Forbearing,
> Most Forgiving!" (Qur'ān, 17:44)

Here we can refer to a Qur'ānic example. The *fiṭrah* (nature and essence of being "human" or the primordial norm of being "human") is an eternal "Trust" (*amānah*) which seeks the presence of the Absolute. *Fiṭrah* would lose its transparent nature by forgetfulness (*ghaflah*) of the presence of the Absolute. In Islamic mysticism, *fiṭrah* resembles a lucid mirror which has to be ceaselessly cleansed of the dust of forgetfulness. God invites the human being to *experience* this *tradition* of purification in the *sanctity* of His presence by turning the very essence of his/her *fiṭrah* towards Him. In so doing, in the experience of annihilation and subsistence, i.e., in the profound level of cosmic awareness, the mystic sees every particle of the cosmos and tangible nature in the pathway of *return*. Turning his/her face (his/her established spiritual perseverance) away from every forgetfulness, the mystic intuits the returning chant of the elements of corporeal nature.

> So set thou thy face
> Truly to the religion being upright,
> The nature in which
> Allāh has made mankind
> No change (there is)
> to the work (wrought)
> By Allāh: that is
> The true Religion
> But most among mankind
> Know not. (Qur'ān, 30:30)

This "eternal essence of being human" (*fiṭrah*), reminds us of the fact that all states (*aḥwāl*) and stations (*maqāmāt*) of the "spiritual path" (*ṭarīqa*) are prepared to make mankind much closer to his/her perfection. This path of "seeking perfection" (*istikmāl*) is an *eternal* path and is tantamount to the eternal return toward the Absolute. In this eternal path, the mystic *never* departs from his/her very essence of being human, even in the ultimate experience of annihilation and subsistence. In this view of *fiṭrah*, the whole cosmos has been created as the bounty for the human being in order to develop his/her perfection. Then, the "mystical path" (*ṭarīqa*) is indeed the "eternal path of human perfection."

Professor Izutsu, properly stated that the "experience of *fanā'* (mystical annihilation) is certainly a human experience," but he may not be correct in stating that "[*fanā'*] *is not solely a human experience. For when he does experience it, he is no longer himself.*" Perhaps it would be better to say that: "*fanā' is solely a human experience, because when he/she does experience it, he/she is more himself/herself*" (closer to his/her perfection, i.e., closer to his/her proper place in the cosmos, and more advanced along the eternal path of perfection which is the path of eternal return towards the Absolute).

It is worth mentioning that in the view of Islamic spirituality, no human being reaches the end of the path of perfection, because always and eternally there is another stage of perfection (another manifestation of the Absolute) ahead which has to be experienced. There is no end to the path of perfection. The manifestations of the Absolute (sanctity) are eternal and infinite and so too the path of human perfection. Within this awareness of his/her eternal ability and quest for perfection, the Islamic mystic never experiences the bitter taste of nihilism.

For the Islamic mystic, testimony to the Unity "*tawḥīd*," based on the Qur'ānic understanding is the essence of each experience, every intention and deed: "*Unto Allāh belong the East and the West and where ever you turn, there is Allāh's Face. Lo! Allāh is All embracing. All knowing.*" (Qur'ān, 2:115).

The mystic, in the profound station of *fanā'* through the constant unveiling of the whole cosmos, continuously embraces the effusions of *tawḥīd* (Unity) of the Absolute. Throughout this station, the mystic simultaneously experiences *baqā'* (subsistence in the Absolute's manifestation).

In this perpetual blend, the mystic witnesses the ceaseless, aimful movement and *return* of the whole cosmos towards the Absolute Existence: "*...Lo! We are Allāh's and unto Him we are returning.*" (Qur'ān, 2:156). In the return towards the Absolute (*istirjā'*), all three dimensions of *sanctity*, *tradition* and *experience* meet with their substantial affinities.

2. Man and Cosmos in the Experience of Return

In Islamic mysticism, *return* towards the Only Absolute Existence is the core doctrine of the eternal journey of the mystics. In the experience of the mystical stations of *annihilation* and *subsistence*—as it was shown above—one is able to see that the nature of *istikmāl* (seeking perfection) in Islamic mysticism is tantamount to the very essence of the *return* towards Him.

The Unity (*tawḥīd*) of the Absolute, with His peerless

Attributes, distinguishes the very heart of the concept of return in Islamic mysticism from other mystical traditions.

> "He is the First and the Last, and the Outward and the Inward; and He is the Knower of all things."(Qur'ān, 57:3).

In the infinite realm of *tawḥīd* (Unity), all aspects of the mystic's daily and spiritual life are connected with the concept of return towards the Only Reality (*Ḥaqq*, *Ḥaqīqah*). Rūmī declares:

> What is to learn the knowledge of God's Unity
> (*tawḥīd-i Khodā*)?
> To consume yourself (*khīsh-tan*) in the presence of
> the One (*Wāhid*).[54]

In the universal remembrance (*dhikr*) of Allāh, the whole cosmos supplicates His Names and returns towards Him.

> "Seest thou not that it is Allāh Whose praises all beings in the heavens and on earth do celebrate, and the birds (of the air) with wings outspread? each one knows its own (mode of) prayer and praise. And Allāh knows well that they do."(Qur'ān, 24:41)

The mystic, by observing the unveiled "essences" (*dhawāt*) of the cosmos, sees this intrinsic quest and movement of the cosmos towards the Absolute Existence.

> This world is one thought [emanating] from the
> Universal Intellect
> The Intellect is like a King, and the manifestations
> (*ṣūrat-hā*) [are His] envoys (*rosol*).[55]

In the eternal experience of *return*, man as the nexus of the whole cosmos, with the Absolute Existence, journeys in the Light of the Absolute's Attributes towards the paragon of the *universal/perfect human being*. The great and eternal responsibility of being *human* (*insān*) has been portrayed in the Qur'ān, when man accepts the great Trust (*amānah*) of the Absolute after the whole creation had refused to accept that ponderous duty. This pivotal verse reminds us of the *cognizant cosmos* which decrees its interconnected, and intelligent (*mush'ir*) nature. The Trust which man willingly embraced is the perpetual love of the Absolute (i.e., the return towards Him). The human being with his/her most exalted nature (*fiṭrah*) among all of God's creatures, is the only one who can represent both macrocosm and microcosm. By embracing this responsibility, the human being becomes the medium for saving the bounties and harmony of the cosmos.

> "We did indeed offer
> The Trust to the Heavens
> And the Earth
> And the Mountains;
> But they refused
> To undertake it,
> Being afraid thereof:
> But man undertook it..." (Qur'ān, 33:72)

The great 14th century Persian mystic and poet, Ḥāfiẓ of Shirāz, portrays this Qur'ānic notion in his *dīwān*:

> For Heaven's self was all too weak to bear
> The burden of His love God laid on it.
> He turned to seek a messenger elsewhere
> And in the Book of Fate my name was writ.[56]

In the path of *return*, the mystic continuously bridles his "*inciting soul* (*nafs-al ammāra*)"[57] and nourishes the awareness of his "*blaming soul* (*nafs-al lawwāma*),"[58] until he attains the certainty of the "*soul at peace* (*nafs-al muṭma'inna*)."[59]

It is not accidental that the term *iṭmi'nān* (peace), also means *certainty*. Therefore, *nafs-al muṭma'inna*, is the soul, which in the *transcendental peace* encompasses the realms of mystical certainty (*yaqīn*). Beyond the twinkling shadows of falsities and doubtfulness, the mystic's soul embraces the quintessence of the Absolute's manifestations. The Divine Reality calls the *soul at peace* to return to *His Heaven of Certainty*.

> "O, (thou) soul at peace (*nafs-al muṭma'inna*)
> Return unto your Lord, well pleased (thyself), and
> well pleasing unto Him!
> Enter you among My devotees!
> Enter you My Heaven!"(Qur'ān, 89:27-30)

Without understanding the concept of "return," the ties between the human being and cosmos remain unclear. *Sanctity*, in the Islamic mystical *tradition*, remains the boundless domain of the "cosmic sovereignty," and the birth place of the mystical *experience* and the whole existence of the mystic. Within the bounties of this atmosphere, Islamic mystics smell the transcendental aroma of their "experience" (i.e., the return).

Conclusion

In studying Islamic mysticism, and its view of the cosmos, nature and the environment, refined symbols and metaphors in the words and experiences of each master, provide us with a picture within which the mystic expresses the meaningful orders and cosmic rules of the whole creation.

Natural and environmental symbols in the mystic's view, do not project an imaginary and fictional view of nature. At the same time, all physical manifestations and the mystical observations of the environment, without any contradiction, penetrate the mystic's heart as manifestations of the Absolute. The noble vision of the mystic in observing nature and the environment in the infinite domain of their Origin, prevents him/her from both blind naturalism and rejection of nature and the environment as symbols of attachment or suffering. In other words, for the mystic, symbolism is understood as an organic and important instrument of *sacralization* of the cosmos and environment. The 14th century Sufi master, Shaykh Maḥmūd Shabistarī declares,

> The world is like you, a person
> You are its soul and it is your body.[60]

Blending his/her gnosis (*ma'rifah*) with the concept of Unity (*tawḥīd*), the mystic in observing the harmonious principles of nature and the environment, realizes the essential passion of the whole existence in its sacred journey towards the One. Performing his/her duty as a believer, the mystic protects this "sacred harmony." This harmony attains the essence of its sacredness from the manifestation of the Absolute's Essence (*dhāt*), which itself is the "sancity." The mystic views the whole cosmos as one sacred consciousness in which "sanctity" defines itself within its continual Unity, and in this way, the perpetual *tradition* of "*seeing only the One everywhere*" continues. Ibn 'Arabī conveys,

> The Breath of the All-merciful is the substance of the engendered *things*. That is why God describes Himself by attributes that belong to temporally originated things, attributes which are considered impossible by rational and considerative proofs...The substance of the cosmos is All-merciful Breath, within which the forms of the cosmos become manifest.[61] [emphasis added]

Throughout our discussion around the relationship between different aspects of the two higher stations of mystical annihilation (*fanā'*) and subsistence (*baqā'*), in addition to the overlapping mystical states and stations, *with* the mystic's observance of nature, the environment and the cosmos, it is hoped that some light has been shed on the use of symbols. The mystic, through these symbols, is able to view both the exoteric and esoteric domains of nature and the environment. Islamic mystics, by applying natural and cosmic symbols and metaphors, reveal their yearning for the unveiling of the real essence (*dhāt*) of the "things" and follow the Prophetic saying (*ḥadīth*) of "*Ilāhī arin al-ashyā' kamā hya*." (O Allāh, show us the entities as they really are). This approach makes the quintessence of the mystic's experience of the "things" within the cosmos and the cosmos as a whole, much closer to its essential reality. Indeed, the mystic comes to the practical realization of the Divine origin of things by being "witness" (*shāhid*) to their real essence. It is worth mentioning that the word *shahādah* (the testimony to the Unity of Allāh in the daily Islamic rituals) and *shāhid* (witness) which is also a mystical term and *shahīd* (martyr) are from the same etymological root (*sh-h-d*). Saying *Shahādah* is also part of the obligatory ritual for every one who wants to become a Muslim. This might be an indicative assertion that one significant spiritual dimension of Islam is to provide the opportunity of being witness to the whole cosmos returning to its Only Source, with man being its creature *par excellence*.

By looking at the whole of nature, environment and the cosmos as the sacred signs of God and as a completely correlated living organism which is an effusion of the One, the mystic realizes that in these exact and delicate series of the Absolute's manifestations, any abusive action within nature and the environment will hurt the whole organism.

The mystic recognizes the Absolute as the only Real Existence from whose Light the whole of existence perpetually receives life. Through this understanding, natural and environmental symbols in the mytical texts reveal the Divine, ontological, external and internal aspects of nature and the environment. In the heart of this collective perspective which manifests itself in the words of Islamic mystics, each cosmic and natural element finds its real place and role in the real order of things. This appears to the mystic as the "most perfect order" (*niẓām-i aḥsan*).

> This world is the mountain, and our action the shout
> The echo of the shouts comes [back] to us.[62]

When the dust, the tree, the water, the moon, and the sun

remind the Islamic mystic of the epiphanies of the Truth, all of nature and the environment will be protected by the believer gardeners!

The intricacy and complexity of a mystical experience remind us of the profound and correlated domains from tradition, history, and culture to etymology and terminology, as well as the implications of the relevant sects, fraternities and local peculiarities—*the required prerequisites*—which lie behind the outward embodiment of a mystical tradition.

The "how" of the interpretation, in the widespread rudiments of these attuned prerequisites, contours the inference, persistence and legitimacy of an analysis of a mystical experience. The very essence of a mystical experience, stores an "*organic identity*" which distinguishes the nature of the ties between that experience and a particular mystical tradition.

An analysis of this interwoven identity is too complicated or too organic to be comprehensible by the mechanical and compartmentalized elements of the *Hobbesian triangle* (*consequent, antecedent and concomitant*). In this realm, Smart's *epoche'*, also, would not be beneficial, until, it comprises the extensive extent of this identity. Therefore, any type of solely mechanical approach to the mystical concepts in Islam is unable to grasp the substantial interdependence which exists between different elements of the organic identity of each Islamic mystical concept.

Considering the shortcoming of a solely mechanical methodology in observing the organic identity of Islamic mystical concepts, this work suggested an *organic methodological triangle* for analysis of the mystical concepts within Islamic mysticism. In the suggested methodological triangle (which includes the three dimensions of sanctity, tradition and experience), "sanctity" inspires the two domains of mystical tradition and mystical experience. By depriving the very essence of the "organic identity" of the mystical experience, from its sanctified linkages *with* a specific "tradition,"conventional scholarship on Islamic mysticism transmutes the contextuality of the "mystical experience" into a series of hollowed performances. "Sanctity" stands at the nurturing point of the suggested methodological triangle which draws a bilateral connection with the "tradition" and "experience." In the affinities between these three dimensions, "sanctity" as the absolute presence of the Absolute (i.e., His manifestations) becomes the *raison d'etre* and the "only domain" of the mystical "experience."

The mystical *tradition* of Islam, which has been nourished directly from the Qur'ān and the tradition of the Prophet of Islam (which in Shi'ī Islam also includes the tradition of Shi'ī Imams and the Prophet's daughter Fāṭimah) as its substantial sources, has been shown by the Islamic mystics to be also included with the whole genealogy of the Semitic prophets. The prominent and respected appearance of such prophets like Jesus, Moses, Abraham, Jacob, Joseph, and Noah in the Islamic mystical texts of different eras are the examples of these ties.

"The mystical *experiences*" of Islamic mystics as the third dimension of the triangle, which reflect the different dimensions of the mystical tradition of Islam, take place in the domain of "sanctity."

Return—"seeking perpetual return to the Origin"—(*istirjā'*), as the essential theme in Islamic mysticism, also manifests its significance in the mystical views on nature, environment and cosmos. One of the shortcomings of contemporary studies in Islamic mysticism lies in the unawareness of the perpetual presence of "return" in each mystical concept. *For the Islamic mystic, the return is not only just a specific moment, but all moments are specifically for return towards the Absolute.* Regarding the centrality of the concept of return in Islamic mysticism and its constant presence in the three dimensions of the suggested triangle, this concept has been employed throughout this work as the *examiner* of the triangle.

In order to demonstrate the function of this suggested methodological triangle, I have chosen the two major stations of the mystical path (*ṭarīqa*), annihilation and subsistence (*fanā'* and *baqā'*). These two have been adopted as the *traditional* framework throughout the work. These two mystical stations are embedded in the very heart of the Islamic mystical tradition, and being the higher stations of the mystical path, help us to observe the other overlapping states (*aḥwāl*) and stations (*maqāmāt*).

Throughout this work, I have tried to elaborate the constant relation of man and cosmos, nature and environment in Islamic mysticism by using a number of Qur'ānic verses, Prophetic traditions and the words of Islamic masters of different eras. The mystic in his/her different levels of awareness regarding cosmos, nature and environment, obtains different levels of affinities with these concepts. *Sayr*, "the horizontal observation of believers in nature and environment," for the mystic, soon becomes a *sulūk* or "constant vertical journey towards the Absolute" in which he/she sees the cosmos, nature and environment as a whole. [Figure 6]

The mystic's ceaseless passion for reaching the station of the universal/perfect human being establishes his/her spiritual perseverance in the path of *istikmāl*, the "eternal quest for perfection," which is the reality of *istirjā'* or "seeking perpetual return towards the Absolute" in the mystical path (*ṭarīqa*). The profound level of cosmic awareness (*ishrāf-i kullī*) in the stations of annihilation and subsistence (*fanā'* and *baqā'*) provides the mystic with an all-encompassing tie with both cosmos and the Absolute. In this level he/she sees the unveiled particles of nature, cosmos and the environment in their proclamation of *tawḥīd* (the Unity the Absolute). In the stations of *fanā'* and *baqā'*, the mystic's utterance of the Unity elevates the proclamation of the whole cosmos to the higher level. The poverty and destitution of the whole cosmos towards the Absolute appears to the mystic as the crying of the whole cosmos for the renewal through return.

The constant re-creation (*khalq-i mudām*) and transubstantial motion (*ḥarakat al-jawhariah*) of each essence (*dhāt*) and accident (*'araḍ*) of the whole cosmos are the manifestations of the absolute poverty (*faqr-i kāmil*) of the whole cosmos in relation to the Absolute, which needs to be fulfilled within the infinite richness of the only Real Content (*Ghanī*). The mystic by facing his/her "primordial nature" (*fiṭrah*), towards the Absolute is the most zealous citizen of the cosmos to manifest this poverty. In the path of perpetual perfection, which is the reality of the Islamic mystical path, and in the profound stations of *fanā'* and *baqā'*, the mystic orchestrates the return of the whole *wujūd* (existence) towards the Absolute *Wujūd* (the Absolute Existence).

Through the perfect human being (*insān al-kāmil*) as the "single goodly word" (*kalimat'un ṭayyibah*), the whole cosmos becomes a "goodly tree" (*shajart'un ṭayyibah*) which is connected to the "Lote-tree of Heaven" (*sidrat'ul muntahā*). [Figure 7]

The mystic, as the representation of the single sacred consciousness of the whole cosmos, perpetuates the *tradition* of perfection in the *experience* of *sanctity*.

The experience of cosmos, nature, and environment within Islamic mysticism could be a proper witness of the organic and flexible nature of the suggested methodological tool, where all three domains of *sanctity, tradition and experience* meet in a united and organic triangle. In a symbiotic meeting of these three dimensions, the language of mysticism, with all its capabilities and limits, delineates a clearer outline of the *organic identity* of the mystical experience.

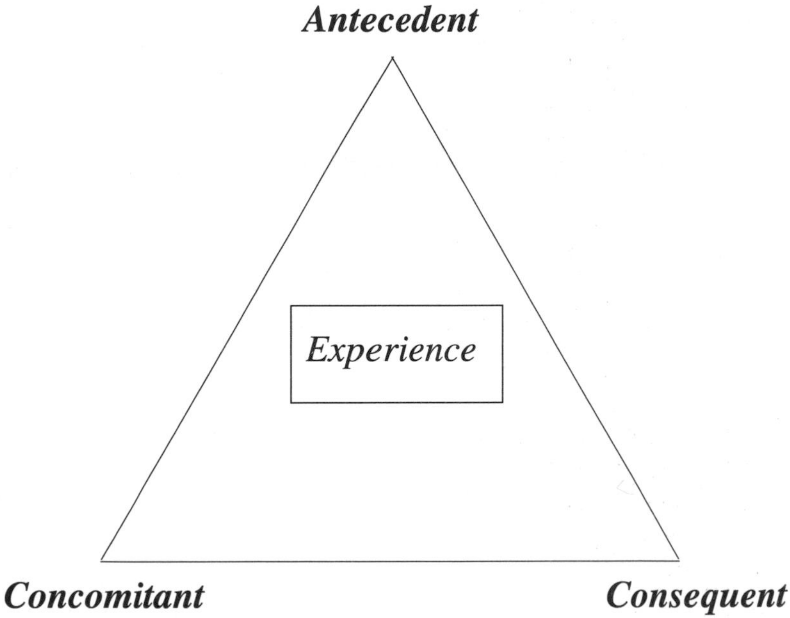

Figure 1

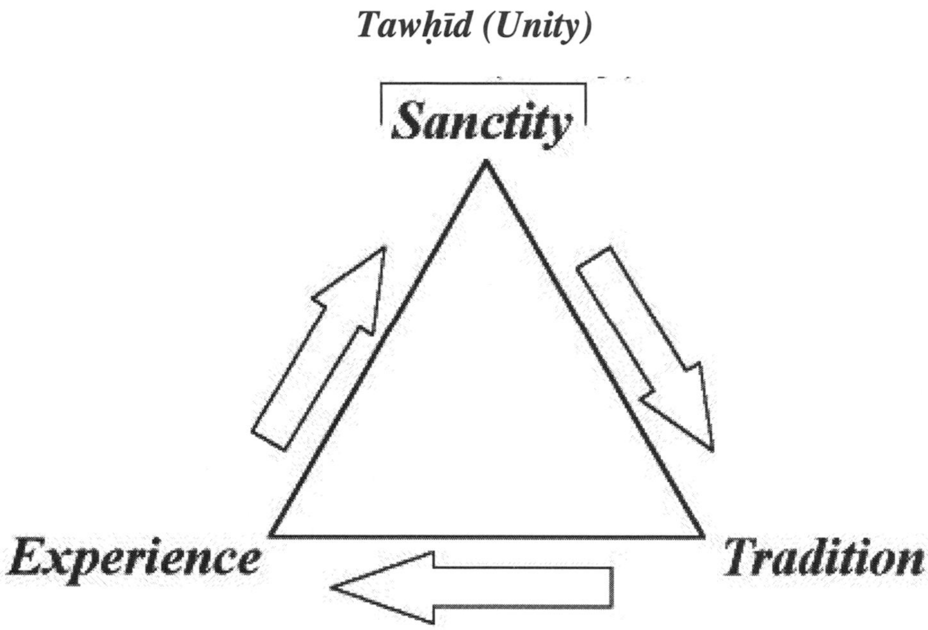

Figure 2

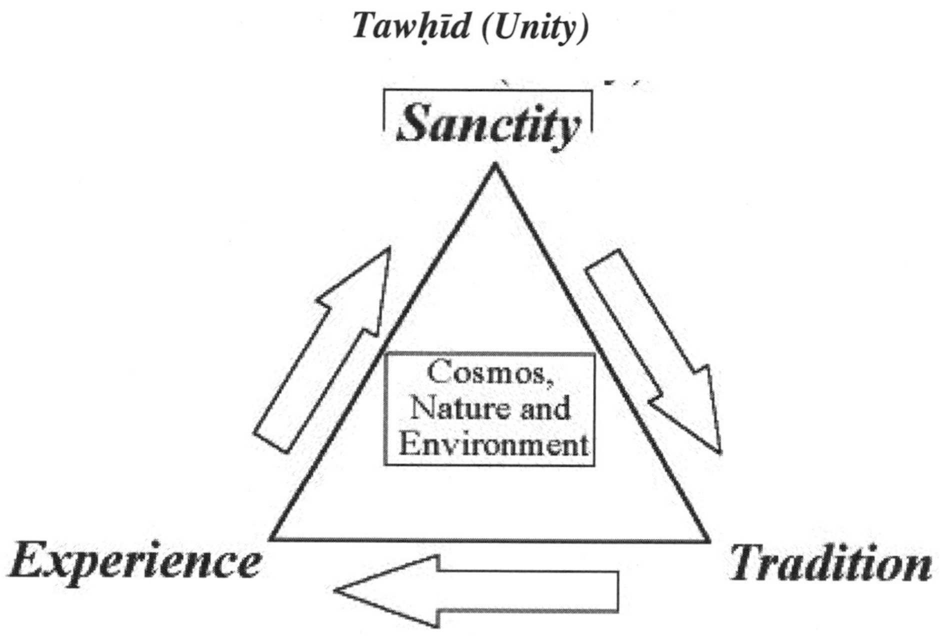
Tawḥīd (Unity)
Sanctity
Cosmos,
Nature and
Environment
Experience
Tradition

Figure 3

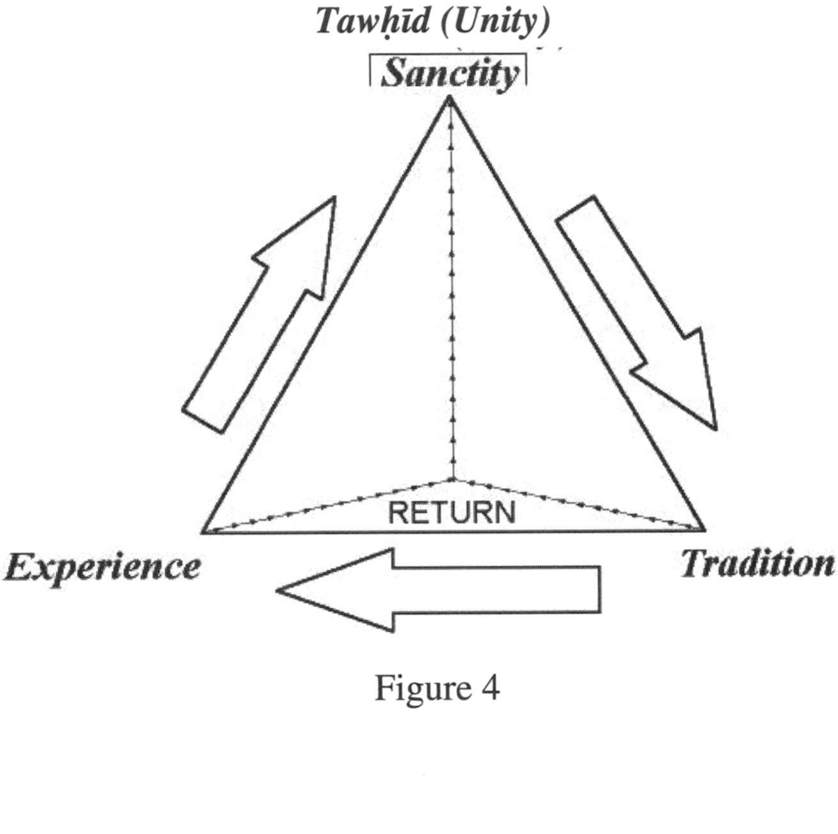

Figure 4

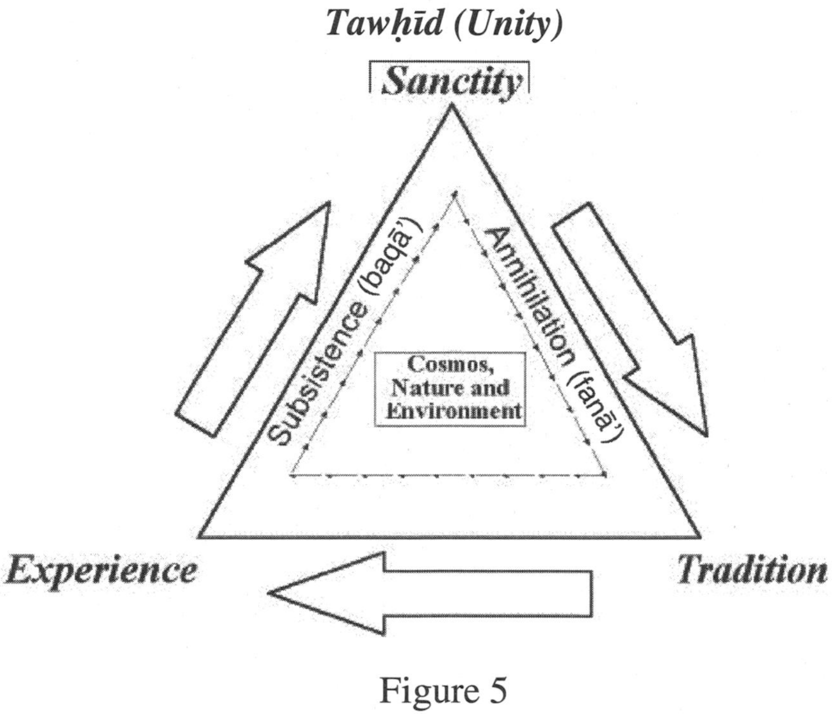
Tawḥīd (Unity)
Sanctity
Subsistence (baqā')
Annihilation (fanā')
Cosmos, Nature and Environment
Experience
Tradition

Figure 5

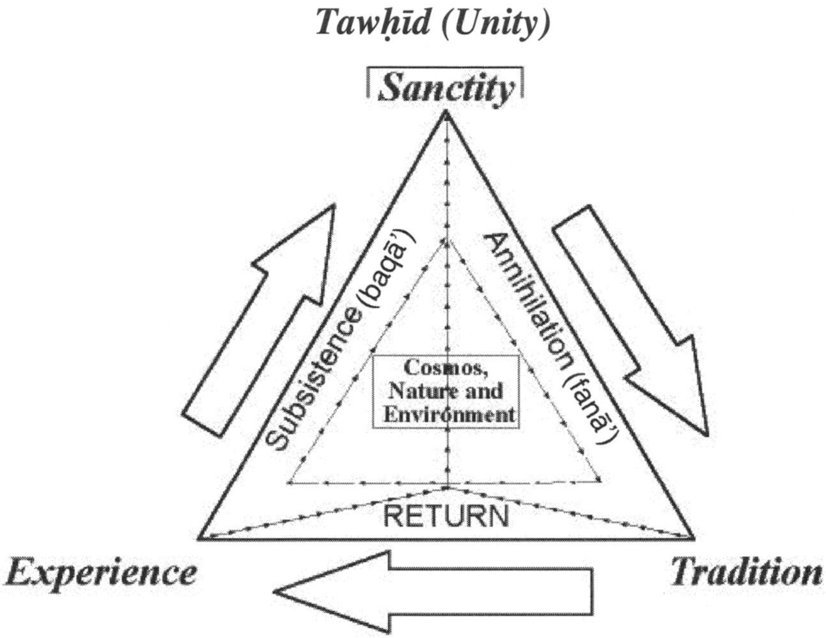
Tawḥīd (Unity)
Sanctity
Subsistence (baqā')
Annihilation (fanā')
Cosmos, Nature and Environment
RETURN
Experience
Tradition

Figure 6

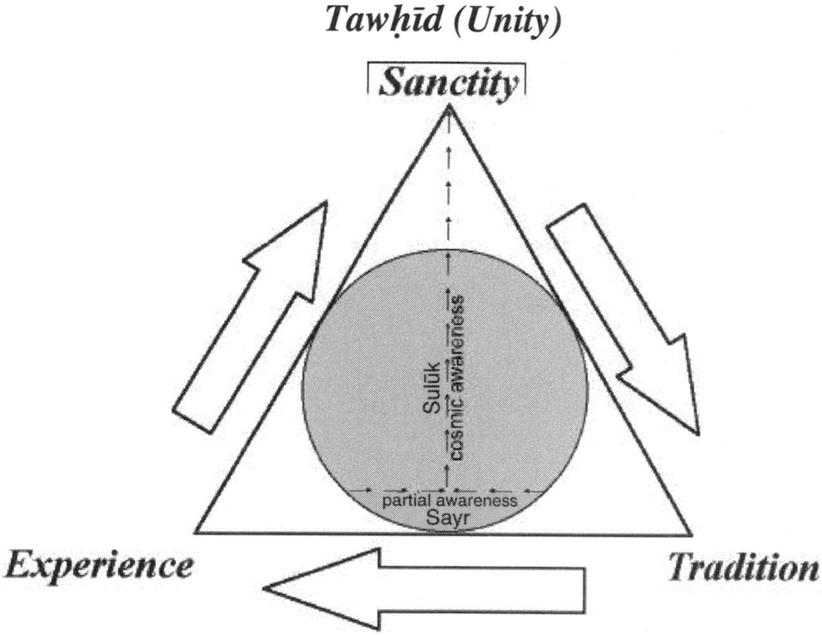
Tawḥīd (Unity)
Sanctity
Sulūk
cosmic awareness
partial awareness
Sayr
Experience
Tradition

Figure 7

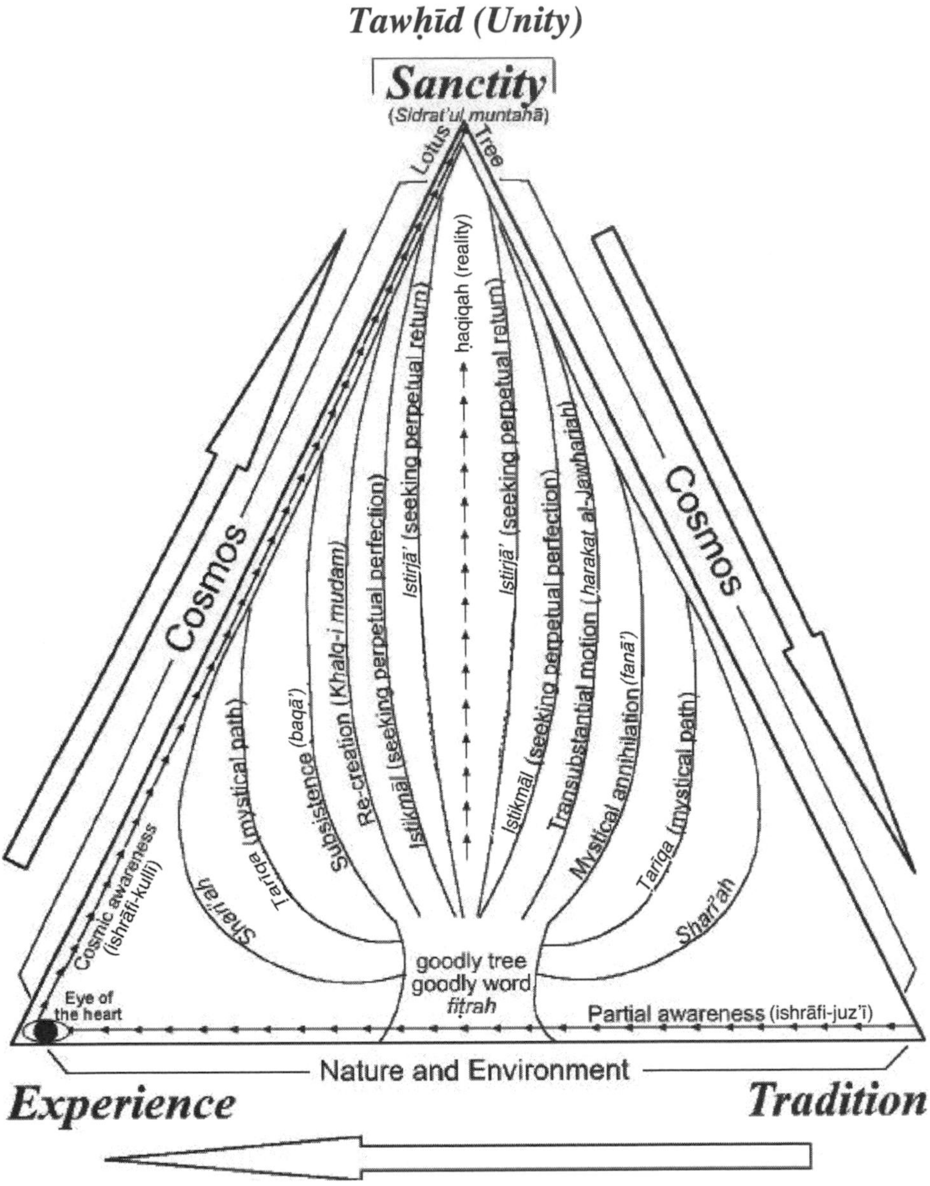
Tawḥīd (Unity)
Sanctity
(Sidrat'ul muntahā)
Lotus Tree
ḥaqiqah (reality)
Istirjā' (seeking perpetual return)
Istirjā' (seeking perpetual return)
Istikmāl (seeking perpetual perfection)
Istikmāl (seeking perpetual perfection)
Re-creation
Subsistence (Khalq-i mudam)
Transubstantial motion (ḥarakat al-Jawhariah)
Subsistence (baqā')
Mystical annihilation (fanā')
Tariqa (mystical path)
Tariqa (mystical path)
Shari'ah
Shari'ah
Cosmos
Cosmos
Cosmic awareness (ishrāfi-kulli)
goodly tree
goodly word
fiṭrah
Eye of the heart
Partial awareness (ishrāfi-juz'ī)
Nature and Environment
Experience
Tradition

Figure 8

Notes

1. George Shelton, *Morality and Sovereignty in the Philosophy of Hobbes* (New York: St. Martin's Press, 1992), pp.11-12 . For further discussion of "experience," see, for example, Immanuel Kant, *Critique of Practical Reason* (Cambridge: Cambridge University Press, 1997), on the "*possibility of experience,*" pp. 38-47; and his *Critique of Pure Reason* (New York: Prometheus Books, 1990), pp. 156-184, where he declares: "*A transcendental use is made of a conception in a fundamental proposition or principle, when it referred to thing in general and considered as things in themselves; an empirical use when it referred merely to phenomena, that is to objects of a possible experience.*" On the issue of "*experience of things past,*" see Rudiger Safranski, *Martin Heidegger: Between Good and Evil*, trans. Ewald Osers (Cambridge: Harvard University Press, 1999), pp. 81-82. On the concept of "*experience in religious way of knowing,*" see William B.Williamson, *Decisions in Philosophy of Religion* (Buffalo: Prometheus Books, 1985).

2. Ninian Smart, *The World Views: Cross Cultural Exploration of Human Belief*, third ed.(Princeton: Prentice Hall, 1995), p. 2.

3. Ibid.

4. For the Qur'ānic translations, I have relied on both Yusuf Ali's and M.M. Picktall's translations with some modifications.

5. Rūmī, *Mathnawī*, vol. 1.

6. Ibid., vol. 3.

7. 'Allāmah Seyyed Moḥammad Ḥossein Ṭabāṭabāī, *Tafsīr-i Almīzān,* vol. 12, trans. into Persian by Seyyed Moḥammad Bāqir Mūsawī Hamadānī (Tehran: Bunyād-i 'Ilmi va Fekrī-yi 'Allāmah Tabāṭabā-ī 1376/1997), pp. 75-76.

8. Annemarie Schimmel, *Mystical Dimensions of Islam* (Chapel Hill: University of North Carolina Press, 1975), p. 134.

9. Ibid., p. 142.

10. Massignon, *The Passion of Ḥallāj: Mystic and Martyr of Islam,* vol. 3, translated from French by Herbert Masson (Princeton: Princeton University Press 1982), p. 352

11. Ibid. I have replaced "gust" with "breeze" in the translation cited here.

12. Murtaḍa Muṭahharī, *Ashinā-yi bā 'Ulūm-i Islāmī: An Introduction to Islamic Sciences*, vol. IV, no. 1 (Tehran: Al-Tawḥīd, 136/1986), p. 23.

13. Schimmel, p. 145.

14. Ibid., p. 48. For further reading on different aspects of "prayer," including its mystical characteristics, see, for example, Laleh Bakhtiar, *Moral Healing through the Most Beautiful Names: The Practice of Spiritual Chivalry* (Chicago: The Institute of Traditional Psycho-ethics and Guidance, 1994); Najīb Māyel Heravī, *Andar Ghazal-i Khīsh Nahān Khāham Gashtan* (Tehran: Nashr-i Nei, 1372/1993), especially *sama'* of Bāyazīd Basṭāmī. See also Ibn 'Ata'ullāh and Khwāja 'Abdullah Anṣārī, *The Book of Wisdom/Intimate Conversation* (New York: Paulist Press, 1978); 'Alī ibn al-Ḥusayn Imām Zayn al-'Abidīn (A.S.), *The Psalms of Islam (al-Ṣaḥifat al-Sajjādīya)*, trans. William C. Chittick (Qūm: Anṣariyan Publication, 1987); Imām 'Alī ibn Abī Ṭālib (A.S.), *Nahj' ul-Balāqah*, collected by Abul Ḥassan Moḥammad al-Raḍi Ibn al-Ḥassan al-Mūsavī, ed. Dr. Ṣubḥī al-Ṣāleḥ (Beirut: Kullīyāt al-Ādāb bi al-Jami'at al-Lubnānīyah, 1387 H. /1967); Ḥājj Mīrzā Javād Malekī Tabrīzī, *Al-Murāqibāt*, trans. into Persian by Ibrāhīm Muḥaddith Bandar Rīgī (Qum: Intishārāt-i Akhlāq, 1376/1997); and his other work, *Asrār al-Ṣalāt*, trans. Reẓā Rajab-Zādeh (Tehran: Payām-i Āzādī , 1363/1984).

15. Prophetic tradition (*ḥadīth*), cited in 'Abbās ibn Muḥammad Rīda al-Qummī, *Safinat al-Biḥār*, vol. 2 (Tehran: Kitābkhāna-yi Sanā'yī 1341/1963), p. 378.

16. Al-Ghazālī, *The Niche of Lights—Mishkāt al-Anwār—* trans. David Buchman (Provo: Brigham Young University Press,

1998), pp. 17-18.

17. Ibid., p. 18.

18. Ibid.

19. Carl W. Ernest, *Rūzbīhān Baqlī: Mysticism and Rhetoric of Sainthood in Persian Sufism* (Baskervile: Curzon Press, 1996), p. 85.

20. Ibid.

21. William C. Chittick, *Imaginal Worlds: Ibn al-'Arabī and the Problem of Religious Diversity* (Albany: State University of New York Press, 1994), p. 61. For further reading on Ibn 'Arabī, see, for example, Claude Addas, *Quest For the Red Sulphur: The Life of Ibn 'Arabī* (Cambridge: Islamic Texts Society, 1993), especially the chapters of "Farewell and Ascension"; Moḥsen Jahāngīrī, *Mohyaddin Ibn 'Arabī: Chihra-yi Barjasta-yi Irfān-i Islāmī* (Tehran: Tehran University Press, 1375/1996). See also Alexander D. Kynsh, *Ibn 'Arabī in the Later Islamic Tradition: The Making of a Polemical Image in Medieval Islam* (Albany: State University of New York Press, 1999); William C. Chittick, *The Sufi Path of Knowledge* (Albany: State University of New York Press, 1989); *The Self Disclosure of God: Principles of Ibn al-'Arabi's Cosmology* (Albany: Suny Press, 1998); and *Ibn 'Arabī: Heir to the Prophets*. Oxford: Oneworld Publications, 2005.

22. Rūmī, *Mathnawī*: vol. 3. Nicholson's translation with some modifications.

23. Ibid., vol. 2. Nicholson's translation.

24. Michael Sells, *Early Islamic Mysticism: Sufi, Qur'ān, Mi'raj, Poetic and Theological Writings* (New York: Paulist Press, 1996), p. 132.

25. *Mathnawī*, vol. 2. Nicholson's translation.

For other approaches to the concept of "light" in Islamic mysticism, see, for example, Henry Corbin, *The Man of Light in Iranian Sufism*, trans. Nancy Pearson (London: Shambhala, 1978); John Walbridge, *The Science of Mystic Lights: Quṭb al-Dīn Shīrāzī and the Illuminationist Tradition in Islamic Philosophy* (Cambridge:

Harvard University Press, 1992); John Walbridge and Ḥossein Ẓiāī, trans., *Suhrawardī's The Philosophy of Illumination* (Provo: Brigham Young University Press, 1999).

See also Ẓiāī, Ḥossein, ed. and trans., *Sohravardi's The Book of Radiance* (Costa Mesa: Mazda Publishers, 1998), and *Knowledge and Illumination: A Study of Suhrawardī's Ḥikmat al-Ishrāq* (Atlanta: Scholars Press, 1990); Mehdī Amīn Raẓavī, *Suhrawardi and The School of Illumination* (Richmond: Curzon Press, 1997); and Muḥammad Sharif b. Nizām al-Dīn b. Hiravī, *Anwāriyyah* (Tehran: Amīr Kabīr Publishers, 1358/1980).

26. William C. Chittick, *The Sufi Path of Knowledge* (Albany: State University of New York Press, 1989), p. 97.

27. Ibid., p. 98.

28. Ibid.

29. For further reading on Mullā Ṣadrā's theosophy, see, for example, Seyyed Hossein Nasr, *Ṣadr al-Din Shirāzī and His Transcendent Theosophy: Background, Life and Works* (Tehran: Institute for Humanities and Cultural Studies, 1997), Fazlur Rahman, *The Philosophy of Mullā Ṣadrā Shirāzī* (Albany: State University of New York Press, 1976), Muḥammad Kamal, *Mullā Ṣadrā's Transcendental Philosophy* (Vermont: Ashgate Publishing Company, 2006), and Zailan Morris, *Revelation, Intellectual Intuition and Reason in the Philosophy of Mullā Ṣadrā: An Analysis of the al-Ḥikmat al-'Arshiyyah* (London: Routledge/Curzon, 2003).

30. *Mathnawī*, vol. 2. Nicholson's translation.

31. *Mathnawī*, vol. 2. Nicholson's translation.

32. See William C. Chittick, "The Five Divine Presences: From Al-Qūnawī to Al-Qayṣarī." *Muslim World* 72 (1982): 107-28. See also Seyyed Hossein Nasr, *An Introduction to Islamic Cosmological Doctrines* (Cambridge: Belknap Press of Harvard University, 1964).

33. *Fuṣūṣ al-Ḥikam*, cited in Michel Chodkiewics, *Seal of the Saints: Prophethood and Sainthood in the Doctrine of Ibn 'Arabī* (Cambridge: Islamic Text Society , 1993), p. 70.

34. Jamal J. Elias, *The Throne Carrier of God: The Life and*

Thought of 'Ala' Ad-Dawla As-Simnānī (Albany: State University of New York, 1995), dedication page.

35. *Mathnawī*, vol.1.

36. *Mathnawī*, vol.5. Nicholson's translation with some modifications.

37. *Mathnawī,* vol 3. Nicholson's translation with some modifications.

38. *Mathnawī*, vol. 5. Nicholson's translation with some modifications.

39. Annemarie Schimmel, *Deciphering the Signs of God: A Phenomenological Approach to Islam* (Albany: State University of New York Press, 1994), p. 8.

40. Ibid.

41. Ibid., pp. 8-9.

42. *Mathnawī*, vol. 4. Nicholson's translation.

43. Ibid. vol. 2.

44. Annemarie Schimmel, *Mystical Dimensions of Islam* (North Carolina: University of North Carolina Press, 1975), p.142.

45. See, for example, the discussion of "*wujūd*" in: Toshihiko Izutsu, *The Fundamental Structure of Sabzwārī's Methaphysics*, trans. Seyyed Jalāl al-Dīn Mujtabavī (Tehran: Tehran University Press, 1368/1990).

46. For the connection between the concept of *bidāha* and *wujūd*, see, for example, 'Allāmah Seyyed Muḥammad Ḥossein Ṭabaṭab'ī, *Bidāyat al-Ḥikmah va Nihāyat al-Ḥikmah* (Qum: Mu'assisa al-Nashr al-Islāmī, 1375/1996), p. 10.

47. Ibid.

48. Ibid.

49. William Chittick, *The Self Disclosure of God: Principles of Ibn al-'Arabī Cosmology* (Albany: State University of New York Press), p. 206.

50. Ibid.

51. Ibid.

52. Emile Durkheim, *The Elementary Forms of the Religious*

Life (New York: George Allen and Unwin Ltd, 1961), p. 496.

53. Toshihiko Izutsu, *Creation and the Timeless Order of Things: Essays in Islamic Mystical Philosophy* (Oregon: White Cloud Press, 1994), p. 13.

54. *Mathnawī*, vol. 1. Nicholson's translation. For further reading on Rūmī, see, for example, 'Abdol Ḥossein Zarrīn Kūb, *Pilla Pilla tā Mulāghāt-i Khodā: dar Bāray-i Zendegī, Andīshah va Sulūk-i Mawlanā Jalāl al-Dīn Rūmī* (Tehran: Sherkat-i Intishārāt-i 'Ilmī va Farhangī, 1373/1994); *Baḥr dar Kūzah* (Tehran: Shirkat-i Intishārāt-i 'Ilmī va Farhangī, 1368/1989); *Sir-re Nei,* 2 vols. (Tehran: Shirkat-i Intishārāt-i 'Ilmī va Farhangī, 1368/1989), pp. 87-96. See also J. T. P. De Bruijn, *Persian Sufi Poetry: An Introduction to The Mystical Use of Classical Persian Poetry* (Richmond: Curzon Press, 1997), and William C.Chittick, *The Sufi Path of Love: The Spiritual Teachings of Rūmī* (Albany: State University of New York Press, 1983); *Rūmī and Me: The Autobiography of Shams-i Tabrīzī* (Louisville: Fons Vitae, 2004).

55. Ibid. vol.2. Nicholson's translation with some modifications.

56. Gertrude Bell , trans. *The Teaching of Ḥafiẓ: Selection from the Diwān* (Octagon Press, 1979), p. 25.

57. Qur'ānic expression in 12: 53.

58. Qur'ānic expression in 75: 2.

59. Qur'ānic expression in 89: 27.

60. Shaykh Muḥammad Lāhījī, *Mafātīḥ al-I'jāz fī Sharḥ-i Gulshan-i Rāz*, Introduction by Keyvan Sami'ī (Tehran: Chāp-i Ḥaydarī, 1326/1947), p. 501.

61. *Fuṣūṣ al-Ḥīkam*, cited in William C. Chittick, *The Sufi Path of Knowledge*. pp. 182-183.

62. *Mathnawī*, vol. 1. Nicholson's translation.

Bibliography

Addas, Claude. *Quest For the Red Sulphur: The Life of Ibn 'Arabī*. Cambridge: Islamic Texts Society, 1993.

Al-Ghazālī, Abū Ḥamid. *The Niche of Lights—Mishkāt al-Anwār*. translated by David Buchman. Provo: Brigham Young University Press, 1988.

Arberry, A .J. *Aspects of Islamic Civilization: The Moslem World depicted through its Literature*. Michigan: University of Michigan Press, 1967.

———. trans. *Koran Interpreted.* New York: Macmillan, 1955.

———. *Revelation and Reason in Islam.* London: George Allen & Unwin Ltd., 1965.

Arkoun, Mohammad. *Rethinking Islam*, trans. and ed. Robert D. Lee. Boulder: Westview Press, 1994.

Ashtiyānī, Seyyed Jalāl al-Dīn. *Sharḥ-i Moghaddama-yi Qayṣarī bar Fuṣūṣ al-Ḥikam*. Tehran: Mu'assisa-yi Intishārāt-i Amīr Kabīr, 1370/1991.

——— and Matsubara, Hideichi and Iwami, Takashi and Matsumoto, Akiro. ed. *Consciousness and Reality: Studies in the Memory of Toshihiko Izutsu*. Leiden: Brill, 1999.

Aṭṭār Nishābūrī, Farīd al-Dīn Muḥammad. *Tadhkirat al-Awliyā'*. Edited by Muḥammad Isti'lāmī. Tehran: Zuwwār, 1374/1996.

Ayoub, Mahmoud M. *Islam: Faith and Practice*. Ontario: Open Press, 1989.

———. *The Awesome News: Interpretation of Juz' 'Amma-The last Part of the Qur'ān*. Hiawatha: World Islamic Call Society, 1997.

Bakhtiar, Lāleh. *Moral Healing through the Most Beautiful Names: The Practice of Spiritual Chivalry*. Chicago: The Institute of Traditional Psychoethics and Guidance, 1994.

Baqlī Shirāzī, Rūzbihān. *The Unveiling of Secrets: Diary of a Sufi Master*. Translated by Carl W. Ernst. Chapel Hill: Parvardigar Press, 1997.

———. *Kitāb-i 'Abhar 'al-'Ashiqīn*. Tehran: Intishārāt i Manūchehrī, 1366/1987.

Buehler, Arthur F. *Sufi Heirs of the Prophet: The Indian Naqshbandiyya and the Rise of the Mediating Sufi Shaykh*. Columbia: University of South Carolina Press, 1998.

Burkhardt, Titus. *Introduction to Sufism: The Mystical Dimensions of Islam*. Translated by D. M. Matheson. Wellingborough: Aquarian Press, 1990.

Chittick, William C. *Imaginal Worlds: Ibn al-'Arabī and the Problem of Religious Diversity*. Albany: The State University of New York Press, 1994.

———. *The Sufi Path of Knowledge*. Albany: The State University of New York Press, 1989.

———. *The Self Disclosure of God: Principles of Ibn al-'Arabī's Cosmology*. Albany: The State University of New York Press, 1998.

———. *Faith and Practice of Islam: Three Thirteenth Century Sufi Texts.* Albany: The State University of New York Press, 1992.

———. *Ibn 'Arabī: Heir to the Prophets.* Oxford: Oneworld Publications, 2005.

———. "The Five Divine Presences: From Al-Qūnawī to Al-Qayṣarī." *Muslim World* 72 (1982): 107-28.

———. trans., *Rūmī and Me: The Autobiography of Shams-i Tabrīzī.* Louisville: Fons Vitae, 2004.

———. *The Sufi Path of Love: The Spiritual Teachings of Rūmī.* Albany: State University of New York Press, 1983.

Chodkiewicz, Michel. *Seal of the Saints: Prophethood and Sainthood in the Doctrine of Ibn 'Arabī.* Translated by Liadain Sherrard. Cambridge: Islamic Texts Society, 1993.

Corbin, Henry. *Swedenberg and Esoteric Islam.* West Chester: Swedenberg Foundation, 1995.

———. *Spiritual Body and Celestial Earth: From Mazdean Iran to Shi'ite Iran.* Translated by Nancy Pearson. Princeton: Princeton University Press, 1977.

———. *Alone with the Alone: Creative Imagination in the Sufism of Ibn 'Arabī.* Princeton: Princeton University Press, 1998.

———. *The Man of Light in Iranian Sufism.* Translated by Nancy Pearson. London: Shambhala, 1978.

Cornell, Vincent J. *Realm of the Saint: Power and Authority in Moroccan Sufism.* Austin: University of Texas Press, 1998.

Critchlow, Keith. *Islamic Patterns: An Analytical and Cosmological Approach*. Rochester: Inner Traditions, 1999.

De Bruijn, J. T. P. *Persian Sufi Poetry: An Introduction to The Mystical Use of Classical Persian Poetry*. Richmond: Curzon Press, 1997.

Durkheim, Emile. *The Elementary Forms of the Religious Life*. New York: George Allen and Unwin Ltd, 1961.

Eliade, Mircae. *The Sacred and the Profane: The Nature of Religion*. New York: Harcourt Brace, 1987.

Elias, Jamal L. *The Throne Carrier of God: The Life and Thought of 'Ala' Ad-Dawla As-Simnān*. Albany: State University of New York Press, 1995.

Ernst, Carl W. *Rūzbīhān Baqlī: Mysticism and Rhetoric of Sainthood in Persian Sufism*. Baskerville: Curzon Press, 1996.

Fadiman, James and Frager, Robert. *Essential Sufism*. New York: Castle Books, 1998.

Farhadi, A. G. Ravan. *Abdullah Anṣāri of Harāt (1006-1089): An Early Sufi Master*. Richmond: Curzon Press, 1996.

Godwin, Jocelyn. *Harmonies of Heaven and Earth: The Spiritual Dimensions of Music*. Rochester: Inner Tradition International, 1987.

Gulpinārli, Abdolbāqi. *Mawlāna Jalāl al-Dīn: Zendegāni, Falsafeh, Athār va Gozīdah-yi az Anhā*. Translated into Persian by Dr. Tawfiq Subhānī. Tehran: Pajūhishgāh-i 'Ūlūm-i Insānī va Muṭāli'āt-i Farhangī, 1375/1996.

Gray, Elizabeth T. *The Green Sea of Heaven: Fifty Ghazals from the Diwan of Hafiz.* Introduction by Daryush Shayegan. Oregon: White Cloud Press, 1995.

Gutas, Dimitri. *Avicenna and the Aristotelian Tradition.* Islamic Philosophy and Theology: Texts and Studies, vol. 4. Leiden: E.J. Brill, 1988.

Hāfiẓ, Shams al-Dīn Muḥammad. *Diwān-i Hāfiẓ.* Edited by Bahā' al-Dīn Khorramshāhī. Tehran: Dūstān, 1379/2000

Hiravī, Muḥammad Sharīf b. Niẓām al-Dīn. *Anwāriyyeh.* Tehran: Amīr Kabīr, 1358/1980.

Haught, John F. *The Promise of Nature: Ecology and Cosmic Purpose.* New York: Paulist Press, 1993.

Ḥorr al-'Āmilī, Muḥammad ibn Ḥassan ibn 'Alī ibn Ḥossein. *Al-Javāhir al-Saniyyah fī Aḥadīth al-Qudsīyyah.* Lebanon: Dār al-Hādī, 1401/1981.

Huxley, Aldous. *The Perennial Philosophy.* London: Collins/Fontana, 1985.

Ibn 'Aṭā'ullāh and Anṣārī, Khwaja Abdullāh. *The Book of Wisdom /Intimate Conversation.* New York: Paulist Press, 1978.

Idleman Smith, Jane and Yazbeck Haddad, Yvonne. *The Islamic Understanding of Death and Resurrection.* Albany: State University of New York Press, 1981.

Imam Zayn al-'Abidīn (A.S.), 'Ail ibn al-Ḥusayn. *The Psalms of Islam (Al-Ṣaḥifat Al-Sajjādiya).* Translated by William C.. Chittick. Qum: Anṣariyan Publication, 1365/1987.

Imam 'Ali (A.S.), Ibn Abi Ṭālib. *Nahj' ul-Balaqah.* Collected by Abul Ḥassan Moḥammad al-Raḍi Ibn al-Ḥassan al-Mūsavī. Edited by Dr. Ṣubḥī al-Ṣālih. Beirut: Kullīyāt al-Ādāb bil-Jāmi'at al-Lubnāniyah, 1387/1967.

'Irāqī, Fakhruddīn. *Divine Flashes.* New York: Paulist Press, 1982.

Izutsu, Toshihiko. *Creation and Timeless Order of Things: Essays in Islamic Mystical Philosophy.* Oregon: White Cloud Press, 1994.

———. *The Fundamental Structure of Sabzawari's Metaphysics.* Tehran: Tehran University Press, 1990.

———. *The Concept and Reality of Existence.* Tokyo: Keio Institute of Cultural and Linguistic Studies, 1971.

Jahāngīrī, Muḥsen. *Muhiyal-Dīn Ibn 'Arabī: Chihra-yi Barjasta-yi 'Irfān-i Islāmī.* Tehran: Tehran University Press, 1375/1996.

Jung, C.G. *Modern Man in the Search of a Sou*l. New York: Harcourt Brace, 1933.

Kamal, Muḥammad. *Mullā Ṣadrā's Transcendental Philosophy.* Vermont: Ashgate Publishing Company, 2006.

Katz, Steven T. ed. *Language, Epistemology and Mysticism in Mystical and Philosophical Analysis.* New York: Oxford University Press, 1978.

Kant, Immanuel. *Critique of Practical Reason.* Cambridge: Cambridge University Press, 1997.

———. *Critique of Pure Reason.* New York: Prometheus Books, 1990.

Kāshānī, ʻAbdul Razzāq. *Iṣṭilāḥāt al-Sufiyyah (Farhang-i Iṣṭilāḥāt-i ʻIrfān va Tasawwuf)*. Translated by Muḥammad Khwājavī. Tehran: Inteshārāt-e Mawlā, 1372/1993.

Khwārazmī, Tāj al-Dīn Ḥossein ibn Ḥassan. *Sharḥ-i Fuṣūṣ al-Ḥikam*. Vol .1. Edited by Najīb Māyel Hiravī. Tehran: Intishārāt-i Mawlā, 1368/1989.

Khorramshāhī, Bahā'al-Dīn. *Ghor'ān Shinākht: Mabāḥithī dar Farhang Āfarīnī-yi Ghor'ān*. Tehran: Ṭarḥ-i Naw, 1376/1997.

———. and Anṣārī, Mas'ūd. ed. and trans. *Payām-i Payāmbar*. Tehran: Jāmī, 1376/1997.

Kritzeck, James. *Anthology of Islamic Literature: From Rise of Islam to Modern Times*. New York: Penguin Books, 1964.

Kynsh, Alexander D. *Ibn ʻArabī in the Later Islamic Tradition: The Making of a Polemical Image in Medieval Islam*. Albany: State University of New York Press, 1999.

Lahījī, Shaykh Muḥammad. *Mafātīḥ al-I'jāz fī Sharḥ-i Gulshan-i Rāz*. Introduction by Keyvān Samī'ī. Tehran: Chāp-i Ḥaydarī, 1326/1947..

Lewisohn, Leonard. *Beyond Faith and Infidelity: The Sufi Poetry and Teaching of Mahmud Shabistari*. Richmond: Curzon Press, 1995.

———. ed. *The Heritage of Sufism. Vol. II: The Legacy of Medieval Persian Sufism* (1150-1500). Oxford: One World, 1999.

Lings, Martin. *What is Sufism?* London: Unwin Hyman Ltd., 1988.

———. *The Book of Certainty: The Sufi Doctrine of Faith, Vision and Gnosis*. Cambridge: Islamic Texts Society, 1992.

———. *Symbol & Archetype: A Study of the Meaning of Existence*. Cambridge: Quinta Essentia, 1991.

Malekī Tabrīzī, Hājj Mirzā Javād. *Al-Murāqibāt*. Translated into Persian by Ibrāhīm Muḥaddeth Bandar Rīgī. Qum: Intishārāt-i Akhlāgh, 1376/1997.

———. *Asrār al-Ṣalāt*. Translated by Reza Rajab-Zādah. Tehran: Payām-i Azādī, 1363/1984.

Massignon, Louis. *The Passion of Ḥallāj: Mystic and Martyr of Islam*. vol. 3. Princeton: Princeton University Press, 1982.

———. *Ḥallāj: Mystic and Martyr*. Princeton: Princeton University Press, 1982.

Mashkūr, Muhammad Javād. *Farhang-i Firagh-i Islāmī*. Introduction by Ustād Kāẓim Mudīr Ṣaḥnechī. Mashad: Bunyād-i Pajūhish-hā-yi Āstān-i Ghods-i Razavī, 1372/1993.

Māyel Hiravī, Najīb. *Andar Ghazal-i Khīsh Nahān Khāham Gashtan*. Tehran: Nashr-i Nei, 1372/1993.

Moosā, Ebrāhīm. *Ghazālī and the Poetics of Imagination*. Chapel Hill: University of North Carolina Press, 2005.

Morris, Zailan. *Revelation, Intellectual Intuition and Reason in the Philosophy of Mullā Ṣadrā: An Analysis of the al-Ḥikmat al-'Arshiyyah*. London: Routledge/Curzon, 2003.

Munzavī, 'Alīnaqī and 'Usayrān, 'Afīf. ed. *Nāmahā-yi 'Ain al-Quḍāt Hamadānī*. Tehran: Kitabkhāna-yi Manūchehrī, 1360/1981.

Murata, Sachiko. *The Tao of Islam: A Sourcebook on Gender Relationships in Islamic Thought.* Foreword by Annemarie Schimmel. Albany: State University of New York Press, 1992.

Mutahharī, Murtaḍa. *Ashina-yi bā 'Ulum-i Islāmī* (An Introduction to Islamic Sciences). vol. IV, no. 1. Tehran: Al-Tawḥīd, 1364/1986.

———. *Fundamentals of Islamic Thought: God, Man and the Universe.* Translated from the Persian by R. Campbell. Berkeley: Mizan Press, 1985.

Nasafī, Shaykh Aziz al-Dīn. *Zubdat' al Ḥaqā'īq.* Edited by Ḥāqq Verdī Nāṣerī. Tehran: Ketābkhāna-yi Ẓuhūrī, 1363/1985.

Nasr, Seyyed Hossein. *An Introduction to Islamic Cosmological Doctrines.* Albany: State University of New York Press, 1993.

———. *Knowledge and the Sacred.* Albany: State University of New York Press, 1989.

———. *Man and Nature: The Spiritual Crisis in Modern Man.* London: Unwin Paperbacks, 1990.

———. *The Need for a Sacred Science.* Albany: State University of New York Press, 1993.

———. *Religion and the Order of Nature.* New York: Oxford University Press, 1996.

———. *An Introduction to Islamic Cosmological Doctrines.* Cambridge: Belknap Press of Harvard University, 1964.

———. *Ṣadr al-Dīn Shīrāzī and His Transcendent Theosophy: Background, Life and Works.* Tehran: Institute for Humanities and Cultural Studies, 1997.

Nicholson, Reynold A. *The Mystics of Islam*. London: Routledge and Kegan Paul Ltd., 1963.

Qūnawī, Ṣadrā al-Dīn. *Nafaḥāt al-Ilāhiyah (Mukāshifāt-i Ilāhīyyah)*. Translated and Introduction by Muhammd Khwājavī. Tehran: Intishārāt-i Mawla , 1375/1996.

———. *Kitāb al-Fukūk: yā Kelid-i Asrar-i Fuṣūṣ al-Ḥikam*. Edited, Translated and Introduction by Muḥammad Khwājavī. Tehran: Intishārāt-i Mawlā, 1371/1992.

Quinn, William W. Jr. *The Only Tradition*. Albany: State University of New York Press, 1997.

Qushayrī 'Abdul Karīm Ibn Havāzan. *Risāla-yi Qushayrīyah*. Edited by Badi'al-Zamān Forūzānfar. Tehran: Sherkat-i Intishārāt-i 'Ilmī va Farhanī, 1374/1995.

Rahman, Fazlur. *The Philosophy of Mullā Ṣadrā Shirāzī*. Albany: State University of New York Press, 1976.

Renard, John. *All the King's Falcons: Rūmī on Prophets and Revelation*. Albany: State University of New York Press, 1994.

Ridgeon, Lloyd. *'Aziz Nasafī*. Richmond: Curzon Press, 1998.

Rūmī, Jalāl al-Dīn. *Diwān-i Shams-i Tabrizī*. Introduction by Badi' al-Zamān Forūzānfar. Tehran: Uraman, 1375/1996.

———. *Kitāb-i Fihī ma Fihī*. Edited by Badi' al-Zamān Forūzānfar. Tehran: Mu'assisa-yi Intishārāt-i Amīr Kabīr, 1369/1990.

———. *Mathnawī of Jalālu'ddīn Rūmī*. Edited and translated by Reynold A. Nicholson. Cambridge: E.J.W. Gibb Memorial Trust, 2001.

Safranski, Rüdiger. *Martin Heidegger: Between Good and Evil*. Translated by Ewald Osers. Cambridge: Harvard University Press, 1999.

Sattārī, Jalāl. *Ramz Andishī va Honar-i Ghodsī*. Tehran: Nashr-i Markaz, 1376/1997.

Schimmel, Annemarie. *Deciphering the Signs of God: A Phenomenological Approach to Islam*. Albany: State University of New York Press, 1994.

———. *Mystical Dimension of Islam*. Chapel Hill: University of North Carolina Press, 1975.

———. *Islam: An Introduction*. New York: State University of New York Press, 1992.

———. trans. *Look ! This is Love: Poems of Rūmī*. Boston: Shambhala, 1996.

———. *The Triumphal Sun: A Study of the Works of Jalaloddin Rūmī*. Albany: State University of New York Press, 1993.

———. *I am Wind, You are Fire: The Life and Work of Rūmī*. Boston: Shambhala, 1992.

Sells, Michael A., ed. *Early Islamic Mysticism: Sufi, Qur'ān, Mi'rāj, Poeic and Theological Writings*. New York: Paulist Press, 1996.

Shīrāzī, Ṣadrā al-Dīn (Mullā Ṣadrā). *Al-Ḥikmat al-Muta'āliya fil-Asfār al-Arba'a*. Tehran: Shirkat al-Ma'ārif al-Islāmiyyah, 1378/1999.

Shelton, George. *Morality and Sovereignty in tlhe Philosophy of Hobbes*. New York: St. Martin's Press, 1992.

Simnānī, 'Alā Ad-Dawlah. *Diwān-i Kāmil-i Ash'ār-i Fārsī wa 'Arabī.* Edited by 'Abd al-Rafī' Ḥaqīqat. Shirkat-i Mu'allifīn wa Mutarjimīn-i Irān, 1364/1985.

Smart, Ninian. *The World Views: Cross Cultural Exploration of Human Belief.* Princeton: Prentice Hall, 1995.

———. *The Religious Experience.* Upper Saddle River, NJ: Prentice Hall, 1996.

Smith, Huston. "Is there a Perennial Philosophy?" *Journal of the American Academy of Religion* LV 3 (1987): 553-68.

———. *The World's Religions: Our Great Wisdom Traditions.* New York: Harper Collins Publishers, 1991.

Ṭabāṭabā'ī, 'Allāmah Seyyed Muḥammad Ḥossein, *Tafsir-i Almizān.* Translated into Persian by Seyyed Muḥammad Bāqir Mūsavī Bandar Rīgī. Tehran: Bunyād-i 'Ilmī va Fikriy-i 'Allamah Ṭabāṭabā'ī, 1375/1997.

———. *Bidāyat al-Ḥikmah va Nihāyat al-Ḥikmah.* Qum: Mu'assisa al-Nashr al-Islāmī, 1375/1997.

———. *Usūl-i Falsafah va Ravesh-i Realism.* Vols 1-3. Introduction and Commentary by: Murtaḍa Muṭahharī. Tehran: Daftar-i Intishārāt-i Islāmī, 1365/1986.

Tabrizī, Shams al-Dīn Muḥammad. *Maghālāt-i Shams.* Edited by Ja'far Modarres Ṣādeqī. Tehran: Nashr-i Markaz, 1373/1994.

Takeshita, Masataka. *Ibn 'Arabī's Theory of the Perfect Man and its Place in the History of Islamic Thought.* Tokyo: Institute for the Study of Language and Cultures of Asia and Africa, 1987.

Thrower, James. *Religion: The Classical Theories*. Washington, D.C.: Georgetown University Press, 1999.

Trimingham, J. Spencer. *The Sufi Orders in Islam*. New York: Oxford University Press, 1998.

Turkah Iṣfahānī, Ṣā'in al-Dīn Alī ibn Muḥammad. *'Aql va 'Ishq ya Munāẓirat-i Khams*. Edited by Akram Jawdī Ni'matī. Tehran: Daftar-i Nashr-i Mīrāth-i Maktūb, 1375/1996.

Turner, Victor. *The Ritual Process: Structure and Anti-Structure*. Hawthorne: Aldine de Gruyter, 1969.

Ulfatī Tabrīzī, Sharaf al-Dīn Ḥossein. *Rashf al-Alḥāẓ fī Kashf al-Alfāẓ*. Edited by Najīb Māyel Hiravī. Tehran: Intishārāt-i Mawla , 1362/1983.

Walbridge, John. *The Science of Mystic Lights: Qutb al-Din Shirazi and the Illuminationist Tradition in Islamic Philosophy*. Cambridge: Harvard University Press, 1992

———. and Ziaī, Hossein. trans. *Suhrawardi's The Philosophy of Illumination*. Provo: Brigham Young University Press, 1999.

Werbner, Pnina and Basu, Helene. ed. *Embodying Charisma: Modernity, Locality and Performance of Emotion in Sufi Cults*. London: Routledge, 1998.

Williamson, William B. *Decisions in Philosophy of Religion*. Buffalo: Prometheus Books, 1985.

Witteveen, H.J. *Universal Sufism*. Rockport: Element, 1997.

Zarrīn Kūb, ʻAbdul Ḥossein. *Pilla Pilla tā Molaghāt-i Khodā: dar Bāray-i Zendegī, Andishah va Sulūk-i Mawlānā Jalāl al-Dīn Rūmī.* Tehran: Shirkat-i Intishārāt-i ʻIlmī va Farhangī, 1373/1994.

———. *Baḥr dar Kūzah.* Tehran: Shirkat-i Intishārāt-i ʻIlmī va Farhangī, 1368/1989.

———. *Sir-ri Nei.* Tehran: Shirkat-i Intishārāt i ʻIlmī va Farhangī, 1368/1989.

Ziaī, Ḥossein. ed. and trans. *Sohravardī's The Book of Radiance.* Costa Mesa: Mazda Publishers, 1998.

———. *Knowledge and Illumination: A Study of Suhrawardī's Ḥikmat al-Ishrāq.* Atlanta: Scholars Press, 1990.

Index

W

Y

Z